Simple Pleasures
Tune into NOW!
Sir John Lubbock

Derived by

Beverly A. Potter

RONIN
Berkeley CA

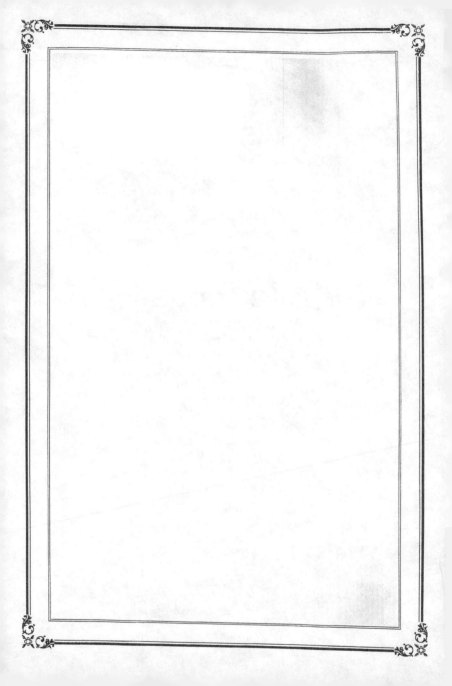

Simple Pleasures
Sir John Lubbock

Derivative by

Beverly A. Potter

Simple Pleasures

Copyright: 2011 by Beverly A. Potter
ISBN: 978-1-57951-119-7

Published by
Ronin Publishing, Inc.
PO Box 22900
Oakland, CA 94609
www.roninpub.com

Library of Congress Card Number: 2011938583
Distributed to the book trade by PGW/Perseus
Printed in the United States

Derived by Beverly A. Potter from *The Pleasures of Life* by Sir John Lubbock.

Table of Contents

Tune into NOW!

Simple Pleasures

*All places that the eye of Heaven
visits are to the wise man ports
and happy havens.*

—Shakespeare

Some murmur, when their sky is clear
And wholly bright to view,
If one small speck of dark appear
In their great heaven of blue.
And some with thankful love are fill'd
If but one streak of light,
One ray of God's good mercy gild
The darkness of their night.

In palaces are hearts that ask,
In discontent and pride,
Why life is such a dreary task,
And all good things denied.
And hearts in poorest huts admire
How love has in their aid
(Love that not ever seems to tire)
Such rich provision made.

—Richard Chenevix Trench

Enjoy Simple Pleasures

Tune into NOW!

Chapter 1

The Duty of Happiness

If a man is unhappy, this must be his own fault; for God made all men to be happy.

— Epictetus

Endeavor to contribute as far as you can to the happiness of your fellow creatures. Be as cheerful as you can, if only because to be happy yourself is a most effective contribution to the happiness of others.

Happiness is more than a selfish desire. It is a moral obligation. You should act as happy as possible.
— Dennis Prager

Happiness ought not to be your main object, nor indeed will it ever be secured if selfishly sought. While you have many pleasures in life, you must not let them have rule over you, or they will soon hand you over to sorrow and into miserable servitude.

A CHEERFUL FRIEND IS LIKE A SUNNY DAY THAT SHEDS ITS BRIGHTNESS ALL AROUND.

Sorrow and joy are strangely interwoven. There is selfish satisfaction in yielding to melancholy and fancying that you are a victim of fate; in brooding over grievances.

> We look before and after,
> And pine for what is not:
> Our sincerest laughter
> With some pain is fraught;
> Our sweetest songs are those
> that tell of saddest thoughts.
>
> — Shelley

YOU CHOOSE TO MAKE OF THIS WORLD A PALACE OR A PRISON.

Keeping yourself happy is an art. Being bright and cheerful often requires effort.

> I have fallen into the hands of thieves. They have left me the sun and moon, fire and water, a loving wife and many friends to pity me, and some to relieve me, and I can still discourse; and, unless I list, they have not taken away my merry countenance and my cheerful spirit and a good conscience.... And he that hath so many causes of joy, and so great, is very much in love with sorrow and peevishness who loses all these pleasures, and chooses to sit down on his little handful of thorns.
>
> — Jeremy Taylor

LIFE IS NOT TO LIVE MERELY, BUT TO LIVE WELL.

Life is a divine gift. Use it wisely. It is your most valuable treasure.

The Privilege of Living

There are some who live without any design at all, and only pass in the world like straws on a river: they do not go; they are carried.

Life must be measured by thought and action, not by time. It certainly may be, and ought to be, bright, interesting, and happy.

If we do our best; if we do not magnify trifling troubles; if we look resolutely, not at the bright side of things, but at things as they really are; if we avail ourselves of the manifold blessings which surround us; we cannot but feel that life is indeed a glorious inheritance.

Few of us realize the wonderful privilege of living or the blessings we inherit; the glories and beauties of the Universe, which is our own if we choose to have it so; the extent to which we can make ourselves what we wish to be; or the power we possess of securing peace, of triumphing over pain and sorrow.

Each of us, as we travel the way of life,
has the choice, according to our working,
of turning all the voices of Nature into
one song of rejoicing; or of withering and
quenching her sympathy into a fearful
withdrawn silence of condemnation—into
a crying out of her stones and a shaking
of her dust against us.

— John Ruskin

Seek not that things should happen as you
wish; but wish the things which happen to
be as they are, and you will have a tran-
quil flow of life....

— Epictetus

A bad mood is a selfish indulence.

How many a day has been damped and
darkened by an angry word!

— St. Bernard

A bad mood is like bad breath. You should
not inflict it upon others.

— Dennis Prager

Happiness begins with maintaining a good
mood.

Happy people make the world better and
unhappy people make it worse.

— Dennis Prager

Whether the life you lead be happy or un-happy is very much in your own power, and depends greatly on yourself.

> **Nothing can work me damage except my-self; the harm that I sustain I carry about with me, and never am a real sufferer but by my own fault.**
> **— St. Bernard**

You are, if not the master, then the creator of yourself. No one was ever made utterly miserable excepting by himself.

> **We are as happy as we decide to be.**
> **— Abraham Lincoln**

It is the little "daily dyings" that cloud over the sunshine of life. Most troubles are in-significant in themselves, and might easily be avoided!

It is your own fault if you are querulous or ill-humored; nor need you allow yourself to be made unhappy by the querulousness or ill-humors of others.

> **The happier you act, the happier you feel.**
> **— Dennis Prager**

Much of what you suffer you have brought on yourself, if not by actual fault, at least by ignorance or thoughtlessness. It is easy to think only of the happiness of the moment, and sacrifice that of the life. Troubles comparatively seldom come to you, it is you who goes to them.

WE FRITTER OUR LIVES AWAY.

We distress ourselves greatly in the apprehension of misfortunes, which after all rarely ever happen.

> **Careworn man has, in all ages,**
> **Sown vanity to reap despair.**
> **— Johann Wolfgang von Goethe**

In trying to save yourself from imaginary or problematical evils, you can incur real suffering.

> **The man who is not content with little is**
> **content with nothing.**
> **— Epicurus**

Most of us give ourselves an immense amount of useless trouble; encumber ourselves on the journey of life with a dead weight of unnecessary baggage;

> **As man maketh his train longer, he**
> **makes his wings shorter.**
> **— Sir Francis Bacon**

Anger does more harm than the thing which makes you angry; and you suffer more from the anger and vexation that you allow to rouse in you, than you do from the acts themselves at which you are angry and vexed.

> I must die. But must I then die sorrowing? Must I be put in chains. Must I then also lament? I must go into exile. Can I be prevented from going with cheerfulness and contentment? ... You may put my body in prison, but my mind not even Zeus himself can overpower.
>
> — Epictetus

CONTENTMENT CONSISTS NOT IN GREAT WEALTH, BUT IN FEW WANTS.

> How is it possible that a man who has nothing, who is naked, houseless, without a hearth, squalid, without a slave, without a city, can pass a life that flows easily?
>
> — Epictetus

Think how much you have to be thankful for. Few appreciate the number of our everyday blessings; rather looking on them as trifles.

Let not the blessings we receive daily from God make us not to value or not praise Him because they be common; let us not forget to praise Him for the innocent mirth and pleasure we have met with since we met together. What would a blind man give to see the pleasant rivers and meadows and flowers and fountains; and this and many other like blessings we enjoy daily.

— Isaak Walton

The world is overflowing with beauty, what more is there to ask for?

Every sort of beauty has been lavished on our allotted home; beauties to enrapture every sense, beauties to satisfy every taste; forms the noblest and the loveliest, colors the most gorgeous and the most delicate, odors the sweetest and subtlest, harmonies the most soothing and the most stirring: the sunny glories of the day; the pale Elysian grace of moonlight; the lake, the mountain, the primeval forest, and the boundless ocean; 'silent pinnacles of aged snow' in one hemisphere, the marvels of tropical luxuriance in another; the serenity of sunsets; the sublimity of storms; everything is bestowed in boundless profusion on the scene of our existence; we can conceive or desire nothing more exquisite or perfect than what is round us every hour; and our perceptions are so framed as to be consciously alive to all. The provision made for our sensuous enjoyment is in overflowing abundance; so is that for the other elements of our complex nature. Who that has revelled in the opening ecstasies of a young Imagination, or the rich marvels of the world of Thought, does not confess that the Intelligence has been dowered at least with as profuse a beneficence as the Senses? Who that has truly tasted and fathomed human Love in its dawning and crowning joys has not thanked God for a felicity which indeed 'passeth understanding.' If we had set our fancy to picture a Creator occupied solely in devising delight for children whom he loved, we could not conceive one single element of bliss which is not here.

— William Rathbone Greg

Chapter 2

The Happiness of Duty

*I am always content with that which happens;
for I think that what God chooses is better
than what I choose.*

— Epictetus

Duty is not a stern taskmistress, as some picture her. Duty is a kind and sympathetic mother, ever ready to shelter you from the cares and anxieties of this world, and to guide you in the paths of peace and fulfillment.

I slept, and dreamed that life was Beauty; I woke, and found that life was Duty.
— Ellen Sturgis Hooper

Your duty is to make yourself useful, and thus life may be most interesting, and yet comparatively free from anxiety. Whereas to shut yourself up from mankind is to lead a dull and selfish life.

The one predominant duty is to find one's work and do it.
— Charlotte Perkins Gilman

You need certainly have no fear of death if you have done your best to make others happy; to promote "peace on earth and goodwill amongst men."

Duty is the most sublime word in our language. Do your duty in all things. You cannot do more. You should never wish to do less.

— **Robert E. Lee**

TO RULE ONESELF IS THE GREATEST DUTY — AND TRIUMPH.

Every duty is a charge, but the charge of oneself is the root of all others.

— **Mencius**

If you give way to yourself, you fall under a most intolerable tyranny. Temptations are in some respects like that of drink. At first, perhaps, it seems delightful, but there is bitterness at the bottom of the cup. Men drink to satisfy the desire created by previous indulgence. So it is in other things.

Repetition soon becomes a craving, not a pleasure. Resistance grows more and more painful; yielding, which at first, perhaps, afforded some slight and temporary gratification, soon ceases to give pleasure, and even if for a time it procures relief, ere long becomes odious itself.

Self-control becomes easier and more delightful. We possess mysteriously a sort of dual nature, and there are few truer triumphs, or more delightful sensations, than to obtain thorough command of oneself.

> **He who is his own monarch contentedly**
> **sways the sceptre of himself, not envying**
> **the glory to crowned heads and Elohim**
> **of the earth.**
> — Sir T. Browne

How much pleasanter it is to ride a spirited horse, even though requiring strength and skill, than to creep along upon a jaded hack. In the one case you feel under you the free, responsive spring of a living and willing force; in the other you have to spur a dull and lifeless slave.

Self-control, this truest and greatest monarchy, rarely comes by inheritance. You must conquer yourself; and you may do so, if you take conscience for your guide and general.

NO ONE REALLY FAILS WHO DOES HIS BEST AND IF YOU HAVE DONE YOUR BEST, YOU WILL HAVE GAINED.

When we have done our best, we should wait the result in peace; content, "with that which happens, for what God chooses is better than what I choose.
— Epictetus

True greatness has little to do with rank or power. A man is his own best kingdom.

He that ruleth his speech is better than he that taketh a city.
— Solomon

The superior man is the man who fulfils his duty.
— Eugene Ionesco

Whether a life is noble or ignoble depends, not on the calling that is adopted, but on the spirit in which it is followed.

It does not matter whether a man "paint the petal of a rose or the chasms of a precipice, so that love and admiration attend on him as he labors, and wait for ever on his work. It does not matter whether he toil for months on a few inches of his canvas, or cover a pal-

ace front with color in a day; so only
that it be with a solemn purpose, that
he have filled his heart with patience,
or urged his hand to haste.
— John Ruskin

The humblest life may be noble, while that
of the most powerful monarch or the greatest genius may be contemptible.

A man who refuses a duty ... is not punished ... but forsaken. And he will never
know love or honor or happiness again.
— S. M. Stirling

Run your own Marathon. You will meet
the Sphinx sitting by the road; to you, as
to Hercules, will be offered the choice of
Vice or Virtue; you may, like Paris, give the
apple of life to Venus, or Juno, or Minerva.

YOU HAVE A GUIDE WITHIN YOU THAT WILL
LEAD YOU STRAIGHT ENOUGH.

You must be sure that you are following a
trustworthy guide, and not out of mere lazi-
ness allowing yourself to drift.

No more duty can be urged upon those who
are entering the great theater of life than
simple loyalty to their best convictions.
— Edwin Hubbel Chapin

> Lead me, O Zeus, and thou, O Destiny.
> The way that I am bid by you to go:
> To follow I am ready. If I choose not,
> I make myself a wretch; —and still must follow.
> — Cleanthes

If you are in doubt what to do, it is a good rule to ask yourself what you will wish to-morrow that you had done today.

RESULTS DEPEND ON THE PREPARATION OF DAILY LIFE.

> Life is made up, not of great sacrifices or duties, but of little things, in which smiles, and kindnesses, and small obliga-tions, given habitually, are what win and preserve the heart and secure comfort.
> — Humphrey Davy

To control your passions you must govern your habits, and keep watch over yourself in the small details of everyday life.

> Ammi says to his son: "Bring me a fruit of that tree and break it open. What is there?" The son said, "Some small seeds." "Break one of them and what do you see?" "Nothing, my lord," "My child," said Ammi, "where you see nothing there dwells a mighty tree."

WATCH YOURSELF IN SMALL THINGS.

It may be questioned whether anything
can be truly called small.
— old Hindoo story

You can, if you will, secure peace of mind
for yourself.

If you wish not to be of an angry tem-
per, do not feed the habit: throw nothing on it which will increase it: at first
keep quiet, and count the days on which
you have not been angry. I used to be
in passion every day; now every second
day; then every third; then every fourth.
But if you have intermitted thirty days,
make a sacrifice to God.

For the habit at first begins to be weakened,
and then is completely destroyed. When you
can say, 'I have not been vexed today, nor
the day before, nor yet on any succeeding
day during two or three months.
— Epictetus

Happy is he who has a sanctuary in his soul.

Men seek retreats, houses in the country, seashores, and mountains: and thou too art wont to desire such things very much. But this is altogether a mark of the most common sort of men; for it is in thy power whenever thou shalt choose, to retire into thyself. For nowhere either with more quiet or more freedom from trouble does a man retire, than into his own soul, particularly when he has within him such thoughts that by looking into them he is immediately in perfect tranquillity.
— Marcus Aurelius

Be careful of what you allow your mind to dwell upon. The soul is dyed by its thoughts; you cannot keep your mind pure if you allow it to be sullied by detailed accounts of crime and sin.

There is no duty we so much underrate as the duty of being happy.
— Robert Louis Stevenson

Life is made up, not of great sacrifices or duties, but of little things, in which smiles, and kindnesses, and small obligations, given habitually, are what win and preserve the heart and secure comfort.
— Humphrey Davy

Chapter 3

The Value of Time

Dost thou love life? Then do not squander time, for that is the stuff life is made of.

—Benjamin Franklin.

What are friends, books, health, the interest of travel or the delights of home, if you have not time for their enjoyment? All good gifts depend on time for their value. Time is often said to be money, but it is more—time is life; and yet many who would cling desperately to life, think nothing of wasting time.

Time is more valuable than money, you can get more money, but you cannot get more time.

— Jim Rohn

How you spend your time is more important than how you spend your money. Money mistakes can be corrected, but time is gone forever.

— David Norris

Hours have wings, fly up to the author
of time, and carry news of our usage....
The misspents of every minute are a new
record against us in heaven.
— John Milton

Time is often said to fly; but it is not so
much the time that flies; we waste it, and
wasted time is worse than no time at all.

I wasted time,

and now doth time waste me.
— Shakespeare

The life of man is seventy years, but how
little of this is actually your own. You must
deduct the time required for sleep, for
meals, for dressing and undressing, for exercise, and then how little remains really at
your own disposal!

Time is the coin of your life. It is the
only coin you have, and only you can de-
termine how it will be spent. Be careful
lest you let other people spend it for you.
— Carl Sandburg

The hours you live for other people, however,
are not those that should be deducted, but
rather those which benefit neither you nor any
one else; which, alas! are often very numerous.

> There are some hours which are taken
> from us, some which are stolen from us,
> and some which slip from us.
> — Seneca

However you lose them, you can never get
them back. It is sad, indeed, how much innocent happiness we thoughtlessly throw away.

TIME IS A SACRED GIFT,
AND EACH DAY IS A LITTLE LIFE.

Suffering may be unavoidable, but no one
has any excuse for being dull. Yet some
people *are* dull. They talk of a better world
to come, while whatever dulness there may
be here is all their own.

> What! dull, when you do not know what
> gives its loveliness of form to the lily, its
> depth of color to the violet, its fragrance
> to the rose; when you do not know in
> what consists the venom of the adder,
> any more than you can imitate the glad
> movements of the dove. What! dull, when
> earth, air, and water are all alike myster-
> ies to you, and when as you stretch out
> your hand you do not touch anything the
> properties of which you have mastered;
> while all the time Nature is inviting you
> to talk earnestly with her, to understand

her, to subdue her, and to be blessed by
her! Go away, man; learn something, do
something, understand something, and let
me hear no more of your dulness.
— Sir Arthur Helps

A great deal of our effort goes into
avoiding death. We make extraordinary
efforts to delay it and often consider its
intrusion a tragic event. Yet we'd find
it hard to live without it. Death gives
meaning to our lives. It gives importance
and value to time. Time would become
meaningless if there were too much of
it. If death were indefinitely put off, the
human psyche would end up, well, like the
gambler in the "Twilight Zone" episode.
— Ray Kurzweil

The more sand that has escaped from
the hourglass of our life, the clearer we
should see through it.
— Jean Paul

Chapter 4

The Wonders of Love

Love rules the court, the camp, the grove,
And men below and saints above;
For love is heaven and heaven is love.

— Sir Walter Scott

Love is the sunshine of life. We humans are so constituted that we cannot fully enjoy ourselves, or anything else, unless some one we love enjoys it with us. Even when alone, we store up our enjoyment in hope of sharing it hereafter with those we love.

There is music in the beauty, and the silver note of love, far sweeter than the sound of any instrument.
— Sir Thomas Browne

Love lasts through life, and adapts itself to every age and circumstance; in childhood for father and mother, in adulthood for spouse, in age for children, and throughout for brothers and sisters, relations and friends. The strength of friendship is proverbial.

Love fills men with affection, and takes away their disaffection, making them meet together at such banquets as these. In sacrifices, feasts, dances, he is our lord—supplying kindness and banishing unkindness, giving friendship and forgiving anmity, the joy of the good, the wonder of the wise, the amazement of the gods, desired by those who have no part in him, and precious to those who have the better part in him; parent of delicacy, luxury, desire, fondness, softness, grace, regardful of the good, regardless of the evil. In every word, work, wish, fear—pilot, comrade, helper, savior; glory of gods and men, leader best and brightest: in whose footsteps let every man follow, sweetly singing in his honor that sweet strain with which love charms the souls of gods and men.

— Agathon

Seeking Your Better Half

The original human nature, acording to Plato, was not like the present. The Primeval Man was round, his back and sides forming a circle; and he had four hands and four feet, one head with two faces, looking opposite ways, set on a round neck and precisely alike. He could walk upright as men now do, backward or forward as he pleased, and he could also roll over and over at a great rate, whirling round on his four hands and four feet, eight in all, like tumblers going over and over with their legs in the air; this was when he wanted to run fast.

Terrible was their might and strength, and the thoughts of their hearts great, and they made an attack upon the gods; of them is told the tale of Otys and Ephialtes, who, as Homer says, dared to scale heaven, and would have laid hands upon the gods. Doubt reigned in the celestial councils. Should they kill them and annihilate the race with thunderbolts, as they had done the giants, then there would be an end of the sacrifices and worship which men offered to them; but, on the other hand, the gods could not suffer their insolence to be unrestrained.

At last, after a good deal of reflection, Zeus discovered a way. He said; "Methinks I have a plan which will humble their pride and mend their manners; they shall continue to exist, but I will cut them in two, which will have a double advantage, for it will halve their strength and we shall have twice as many sacrifices. They shall walk upright on two legs, and if they continue insolent and will not be quiet, I will split them again and they shall hop on a single leg." He spoke and cut men in two, "as you might split an egg with a hair.".... After the division the two parts of man, each desiring his other half, came together....

So ancient is the desire of one another which is implanted in us, reuniting our original nature, making one of two, and healing the state of man. Each of us when separated is but the indenture of a man, having one side only, like a flat-fish and he is always looking for his other half.

When one of them finds his other half, the pair are lost in amazement of love and friendship and intimacy, and one will not be out of the other's sight even for a minute: they will pass their whole lives together; yet they could not explain what they desire of one another. For the intense yearning which each of them has toward the other does not appear to be the desire of lover's intercourse, but of something else, which the soul of either evidently desires and cannot tell, and of which she has only a dark and doubtful presentiment.

Love at first sight.

We often form our opinion almost instantaneously, and such impressions seldom change, I might even say, they are seldom wrong. Love at first sight sounds like an imprudence, and yet is almost a revelation. It seems as if we were but renewing the relations of a previous existence.

> But to see her were to love her,
> Love but her, and love for ever.
> — Robert Burns

The deepest affection is often of slow growth. Many a warm love has been won by faithful devotion.

> Few have married for love
> without repenting it.
>
> — Montaigne

LOVE ENDURES;
IT DEFIES DISTANCE AND ELEMENTS.

Love can be happy anywhere.

> O that the desert were my dwelling-place,
> With one fair Spirit for my minister,
> That I might all forget the human race,
> And, hating no one, love but only her.
> — Byron

Doubtless many have felt

O Love! what hours were thine and mine
In lands of Palm and Southern Pine,
In lands of Palm, of Orange blossom,
Of Olive, Aloe, and Maize and Vine.

— Byron

Popular sayings reveal love's truths.

All women are perfection, especially she
who loves you.

—Turkish Proverb

A woman draws more with a hair of her
head than a pair of oxen well harnessed;"
he answered with a smile, "The hair is unnecessary, woman is powerful as fate.

— Polish proverb

Love is the Angel of Happiness

It is the secret sympathy,
The silver link, the silken tie,
Which heart to heart, and mind to mind
In body and in soul can bind.

— Sir Walter Scott

A friend is even truer than a wife.

> No man that imparteth his joys to his friend, but he joyeth the more; and no man that imparteth his griefs to his friend, but he grieveth the less.
>
> — Sir Francis Bacon

When a beloved comes near, we

> At once it seems that something new or strange
> Has passed upon the flowers, the trees, the ground;
> Some slight but unintelligible change
> On everything around.
>
> — Richard Chenevix Trench

Love and Reason divide our lives. We must give to each its due. If it is impossible to attain to virtue by the aid of Reason without Love, neither can we do so by means of Love alone without Reason.

> Love sowing in the heart of man the sweet harvest of desire, mixes the sweetest and most beautiful things together.
>
> — Melanippides

Love has brought poets many of their sweetest inspirations.

With thee conversing, I forget all time,
All seasons, and their change, all please alike.
Sweet is the breath of morn, her rising sweet
With charm of earliest birds; pleasant the sun
When first on this delightful land he spreads
His orient beams on herb, tree, fruit, and flower
Glistering with dew, fragrant the fertile earth
After soft showers; and sweet the coming on
Of grateful evening mild; then silent night
With this her solemn bird and this fair moon,
And these the gems of heaven, her starry train:
But neither breath of morn when she ascends
With charm of earliest birds, nor rising sun
On this delightful land, nor herb, fruit, flower
Glistering with dew, nor fragrance after showers,
Nor grateful evening mild, nor silent night
With this her solemn bird, nor walk by moon
Or glittering starlight, without thee is sweet.

— John Milton

Love creates love, that even the humblest
may hope for the happiest marriage if only
he deserves it.

She is mine own,
And I as rich in having such a jewel
As twenty seas, if all their sands were pearls,
The water nectar, and the rocks pure gold.

— Shakespeare

Love is delicate. You might as well expect a violin to remain in tune when roughly used, as to expect Love to survive when chilled. But what a pleasure to keep it alive by

> **Little, nameless, unremembered acts**
> **Of kindness and of love.**
>
> — **William Wordsworth**

Love is brittle.

> **The little rift within the lute,**
>
> **Should neither victim be, nor tyrant prove.**
> **Thus shall that rein, which often mars the bliss**
> **Of wedlock, scarce be felt; and thus your wife**
> **Ne'er in the husband shall the lover miss.**
>
> — **Alfred Lord Tennyson**

We are ennobled by true love.

> **Tis better to have loved and lost**
> **Than never to have loved at all.**
>
> — **Alfred Lord Tennyson**

True love grows and deepens with time. Husband and wife, who are married live:

> **By each other, till to love and live**
> **Be one.**
>
> — **Swinburne**

Does love end with death?

They err who tell us Love can die,
With life all other passions fly,
All others are but vanity.
In Heaven Ambition cannot dwell,
Nor Avarice in the vaults of Hell;
Earthly these passions of the Earth;
They perish where they have their birth,
But Love is indestructible;
Its holy flame forever burneth,
From Heaven it came, to Heaven returneth;
Too oft on Earth a troubled guest,
At times deceived, at times opprest,
It here is tried and purified,
Then hath in Heaven its perfect rest:
It soweth here with toil and care,
But the harvest time of Love is there.

— Robert Southey

Mother's love knows no bounds.

The mother when she meets on high
The Babe she lost in infancy,
Hath she not then, for pains and fears,
The day of woe, the watchful night,
For all her sorrow, all her tears,
An over-payment of delight?

— Robert Southey

The love of animals must not be omitted.

Admitted to that equal sky
His faithful dog shall bear him company.

— Alexander Pope

In the *Mahabharata*, the great Indian Epic, when the family of Pandavas, the heroes, at length reach the gates of heaven, they are welcomed themselves, but are told that their dog cannot come in. Having pleaded in vain, they turn to depart, as they say they can never leave their faithful companion. Then at the last moment the Angel at the door relents, and their Dog is allowed to enter with them.

Chapter 5

The Pleasures of Home

There's no place like Home.

— Old English Song

It is such a delight to return home from a thoroughly enjoyed vacation; to find oneself, with renewed vigor, with a fresh store of memories and ideas, back once more by one's own fireside, with one's family, friends, and books.

To sit at home with an old book of romantic yet credible voyages and travels to read, an old bearded traveler for its hero, a fireside in an old country house to read it by, curtains drawn, and just wind enough stirring out of doors to make an accompaniment to the billows or forests we are reading of—this surely is one of the perfect moments of existence.

— Leigh Hunt

It is a great privilege to visit foreign countries; to travel in Mexico or Peru, or to cruise among the Pacific Islands. Narratives of early travelers, the histories of Prescott,

and the voyages of Captain Cook are especially interesting; describing to us, as they
do, a state of society, which was then so
unlike ours, but which has now been much
changed and Westernized.

We may make our daily travels interesting,
even though, all our adventures are by our
own fireside, and all our migrations from
one room to another.

Even if the beauties of home are humble,
they are infinite.

> **Cultivate a talent very fortunate for a
> man of my disposition, that of travelling
> in my easy chair; of transporting my-
> self, without stirring from my parlor, to
> distant places and to absent friends; of
> drawing scenes in my mind's eye; and of
> peopling them with the groups of fancy,
> or the society of remembrance.**
>
> **— Mackenzie**

The succession of seasons multiplies every
home. How different is the view from the
windows as you look on the tender green of
spring, the rich foliage of summer, the glorious tints of autumn, or the delicate tracery
of winter.

Calm mornings of sunshine visit us at times, appearing like glimpses of departed spring amid the wilderness of wet and windy days that lead to winter. It is pleasant, when these interludes of silver light occur, to ride into the woods and see how wonderful are all the colors of decay. Overhead, the elms and chestnuts hang their wealth of golden leaves, while the beeches darken into russet tones, and the wild cherry glows like blood-red wine. In the hedges crimson haws and scarlet hips are wreathed with hoary clematis or necklaces of coral briony-berries; the brambles burn with many-colored flames; the dog-wood is bronzed to purple; and here and there the spindle-wood puts forth its fruit, like knots of rosy buds, on delicate frail twigs. Underneath lie fallen leaves, and the brown brake rises to our knees as we thread the forest paths.

— J. A. Symonds

Each day brings a succession of glorious pictures in never-ending variety. The beauty of the sky is a pleasure. Gray, how it begins with a slight whitening, just tinged with gold and blue, lit up all at once by a little line of insufferable brightness that rapidly grows to half an orb, and so to a whole one too glorious to be distinctly seen.

From the zenith to the horizon, becomes one molten, mantling sea of color and fire; every block bar turns into massy gold, every ripple and wave into unsullied, shadowless crimson, and purple, and scarlet, and colors for which there are no words in language, and no ideas in the mind—things which can only be conceived while they are visible; the intense hollow blue of the upper sky melting through it all, showing here deep and pure, and lightness; there, modulated by the filmy, formless body of the transparent vapor, till it is lost imperceptibly in its crimson and gold.

— John Ruskin

The glorious sky kaleidoscope goes on all day long. Nor does the beauty end with the day.

For my part I always regret the custom of shutting up our rooms in the evening, as though there was nothing worth seeing outside. What, however, can be more beautiful than to "look how the floor of heaven is thick inlaid with patines of bright gold," or to watch the moon journeying in calm and silver glory through the night. And even if we do not feel that "the man who has seen the rising moon break out of the clouds at midnight, has been present like an Archangel at the creation of light and of the world.

— Ralph Waldo Emerson

TRUE PLEASURES OF HOME ARE NOT WITHOUT, BUT WITHIN.

The domestic man who loves no music so
well as his own kitchen clock and the airs
which the logs sing to him as they burn
on the hearth, has solaces which others
never dream of.
— Ralph Waldo Emerson

He is the happiest, be he king or peasant,
who finds peace in his home.
— Johann Wolfgang von Goethe

We love the ticking of the clock, and the
flicker of the fire, like the sound of the cawing of rooks, not so much for any beauty of
their own as for their associations. We call
up what memories.

How dear to this heart
are the scenes of my childhood,
When fond recollection recalls them to view.
The orchard, the meadow,
the deep-tangled wildwood
And every lov'd spot which my infancy knew.
— Samuel Woodworth

Fireside enjoyments,
And all the comforts of the lowly roof.
— William Cowper

Sweet is the smile of home; the mutual look,
When hearts are of each other sure;
Sweet all the joys that crowd the household nook,
The haunt of all affections pure.
— John Keble

Home is a haven of repose from the storms and perils of the world. But to secure this you must not be content to pave it with good intentions, but must make it bright and cheerful.

If your life be one of toil and of suffering, if the world outside be cold and dreary, what a pleasure to return to the sunshine of happy faces and the warmth of home.

Home is the one place in all this world where hearts are sure of each other. It is the place of confidence. It is the place where we tear off that mask of guarded and suspicious coldness which the world forces us to wear in self-defense, and where we pour out the unreserved communications of full and confiding hearts. It is the spot where expressions of tenderness gush out without any sensation of awkwardness and without any dread of ridicule.
— Frederick W. Robertson

The ache for home lives in all of us, the safe place where we can go as we are and not be questioned.

— Maya Angelou

Home is a place you grow up wanting to leave, and grow old wanting to get back to.

— John Ed Pearce

Chapter 6

The Blessing of Friends

*They seem to take away the sun from the
world who withdraw friendship from life;
for we have received nothing better from the
Immortal Gods, nothing more delightful.*

— Marcus Tullius Cicero

In the choice of a dog or of a horse, we exercise the greatest care. We inquire into its pedigree, its training and character. Too often we leave the selection of our friends, by whom our whole life will be more or less influenced for good or evil—almost to chance.

**Every man can tell how many goats or
sheep he possesses, but not how
many friends.**
— Marcus Tullius Cicero

It is wise always to treat a friend, remembering that he may become an enemy, and an enemy, remembering that he may become a friend;

Many people seem to take more pains and more pleasure in making enemies, than in making friends.

He who has a thousand friends,
Has never a one to spare,
And he who has one enemy,
Will meet him everywhere.
— Ralph Waldo Emerson

WHILE THERE ARE FEW GREAT FRIENDS
THERE IS NO LITTLE ENEMY.

There is hardly anyone from whom you may not learn much, if only they will trouble themselves to tell you. Even if they teach you nothing, they may help you by the stimulus of intelligent questions, or the warmth of sympathy.

The happiness and purity of your life depends on your making a wise choice of your companions and friends.

If your friends are badly chosen they will inevitably drag you down; if well they will raise you up.

It is right to be courteous and considerate to every one you meet, but to choose them as real friends is another matter.

Some make a man a friend, or try to do so, because he lives near, because he is in the same business, travels on the same line of railway, or for some other trivial reason. There cannot be a greater mistake. These are only "the idols and images of friendship."

BE FRIENDLY WITH EVERY ONE. THERE IS GOOD IN MOST MEN.

Men talk of unkind hearts, kind deeds
With coldness still returning.
Alas! the gratitude of men
Has oftener left me mourning.
— William Wordsworth

We walk alone in the world. Friends such as we desire are dreams and fables. But a sublime hope cheers ever the faithful heart, that elsewhere in other regions of the universal power souls are now acting, enduring, and daring, which can love us, and which we can love.
— Ralph Waldo Emerson

There is little friendship in the world, and least of all between equals, which was wont to be magnified. That that is, is between superior and inferior, whose fortunes may comprehend the one to the other.
— Sir Francis Bacon

Not only does friendship introduce "day-light in the understanding out of darkness and confusion of thoughts;" it "maketh a fair day in the affections from storm and tempests:" in consultation with a friend a man "tosseth his thoughts more easily; he marshalleth them more orderly; he seeth how they look when they are turned into words; finally, he waxeth wiser than himself, and that more by an hour's discourse than by a day's meditation."... "But little do men perceive what solitude is, and how far it extendeth, for a crowd is not company, and faces are but a gallery of pictures, and talk but a tinkling cymbal where there is no love."

— Sir Francis Bacon

WHEN YOU HAVE MADE A FRIEND, KEEP HIM.

Hast thou a friend visit him often, for thorns and brushwood obstruct the road which no one treads.

— Eastern proverb

Some people never seem to appreciate their friends till they have lost them.

But he who has once stood beside the grave to look back on the companionship which has been for ever closed, feeling

how impotent then are the wild love and
the keen sorrow, to give one instant's
pleasure to the pulseless heart, or atone
in the lowest measure to the departed spirit for the hour of unkindness, will scarcely
for the future incur that debt to the heart
which can only be discharged to the dust.
— John Ruskin

Death does not sever friendship.

Friends, though absent, are still present;
though in poverty they are rich; though
weak, yet in the enjoyment of health;
and, what is still more difficult to assert,
though dead they are alive.
— Marcus Tullius Cicero

If, then, you choose your friends for what
they are, not for what they have, and if you
deserve so great a blessing, then they will
be always with you, preserved in absence,
and even after death, in the "amber of
memory."

Chapter 7

The Pursuit of Health

*Life without health is a burden, with
health is a joy and gladness.*

— Henry Wadsworth Longfellow

There are many who will not take the little trouble, or submit to the slight sacrifices, necessary to maintain their health. They deliberately ruin their health, and incur the certainty of an early grave, or an old age of suffering. They may say, "I suffer, therefore I am."

It is very much your fault that you are ill. You do those things which you ought not to do, and you leave undone those things which you ought to have done, and then you wonder there is no health in you.

YOU KNOW
YOU CAN MAKE YOURSELF ILL.

Perhaps you don't realize how much you can do to keep yourself well. Much of your suffering is self-inflicted due to neglecting the homely precautions by which health might be secured.

Ill-health is no excuse for moroseness. If you have one disease you may at least congratulate yourself that you are escaping all the rest. Many of the greatest invalids have borne their sufferings with cheerfulness and good spirits.

Many have undergone much unnecessary suffering, and valuable lives have often been lost, through ignorance or carelessness.

Considering musicians, what a grievous loss to the world it is that Pergolesi died at twenty-six, Schubert at thirty-one, Mozart at thirty-five, Purcell at thirty-seven, and Mendelssohn at thirty-eight.

It seems nonsensical that so many neglect care over their body, on the state of which happiness so much depends.

The requisites of health are plain enough; regular habits, daily exercise, cleanliness, and moderation in all things—in eating as well as in drinking—would keep most people well.

So much suffering and ill-humor of life is due to over-eating.

To lengthen your life, shorten your meals.
                                    — Old Proverb

It matters little what a healthy man eats, so long as he does not eat too much.

> **Go to your banquet then, but use delight,**
> **So as to rise still with an appetite.**
>   **— Robert Herrick**

Though the rule not to eat or drink too much is simple enough in theory, it is not quite so easy in application.

> **Moreover, it may seem paradoxical, but it is certainly true, that in the long run the moderate man will derive more enjoyment even from eating and drinking, than the glutton or the drunkard will ever obtain. They know not what it is to enjoy "the exquisite taste of common dry bread.**
>   **— Hamerton**

A healthy appetite is a good test of your bodily condition; and indeed in some cases of your mental state.

Cheerfulness and good humor during meals are not only pleasant in themselves, but conduce greatly to health.

What salt is to food, wit and humor are to conversation and literature.

CHERISH YOUR BODY, EVEN IF IT BE A FRAIL AND HUMBLE COMPANION.

Do you not owe to the eye your enjoyment of the beauties of this world and the glories of the Heavens; to the ear the voices of friends and all the delights of music; are not the hands most faithful and invaluable instruments, ever ready in case of need, ever willing to do our bidding; and even the feet bear you without a murmur along the roughest and stoniest paths of life.

With reasonable care, you can hope to enjoy good health. And yet what a marvellous and complex organization your body is! You are wonderfully made.

Strange that a harp of a thousand strings,
Should keep in tune so long.
— William Billings

Considering the marvellous complexity of bodily organization, it seems a miracle that we should live at all; much more that the innumerable organs and processes should continue day after day and year after year with so much regularity and so little friction that we are sometimes scarcely conscious of having a body at all.

With reasonable care you keep your wonderful body in health; so that it will work without causing pain, or even discomfort, for many decades; even when old age come

Time may lay his hand
Upon your heart gently, not smiting it
But as a harper lays his open palm
Upon his harp, to deaden its vibrations.

— Henry Wadsworth Longfellow

Chapter 8

The Comforts of Faith

*Faith is the substance of things hoped
for, the evidence of things not seen.*
— Hebrews 11

Faith rovides a great comfort and support in times of sorrow and suffering,
and a source of the purest happiness.

Religion should be a strength, guide, and
comfort, not a source of intellectual anxiety or angry argument.

Many a man and still more many a woman, render themselves miserable on entering life by theological doubts and difficulties. These have reference, in ninety-nine
cases out of a hundred, not to what we
should do, but to what we should think.

As regards action, conscience is generally a
ready guide; to follow it is the real difficulty.

**For what doth the Lord require of thee,
but to do justly, to love mercy, and to
walk humbly with thy God.**
— Micah 6:8

The differences which keep us apart have their origin rather in the study than the Church. Religion was intended to bring peace on earth and goodwill toward men, and whatever tends to hatred and persecution, however correct in the letter, must be utterly wrong in the spirit.

Knowledge puffeth up, but charity edifieth.
— 1 Corinthians 8:1

Participation in a community of faith can give individuals a sense of connection and belonging that so many of us seek.

Faith is not something to grasp, it is a
state to grow into.
— Mohandas Gandhi

People who disconnect from their faith community—whether because of a move or other life circumstances—often feel a sense of loss. If something is missing from your life, consider reconnecting with the faith or religious practices that you feel can enhance and enrich your spirit.

The Problem of Divine Hiddenness

The felt absence of God – for both believers and nonbelievers – may lead to hopelessness, despair, or indifference.

> **Faith is a necessity to a man. Woe to him who believes in nothing.**
> — Victor Hugo

Evidence of God is available to everyone. However, this available evidence might not be *apprehended* or *perceived* by everyone. If this is true, then the fact that one particular unbeliever sees no evidence for God's existence may be a choice. That is, the use of one's will may block one from "seeing" or "hearing" the evidence of God that is available.

> **He who has faith has... an inward reservoir of courage, hope, confidence, calmness, and assuring trust that all will come out well - even though to the world it may appear to come out most badly.**
> —B. C. Forbes

FAITH PROVIDES STRUCTURE

Faith gives a structure or framework within which to live our lives according to our faith or beliefs.

Many things have been mistaken for religion, selfishness especially, but also fear, hope, love of music, of art, of pomp; scruples often take the place of love, and the glory of heaven is sometimes made to depend upon precious stones and jewelry.

MANY RUN AFTER CHRIST, NOT FOR THE MIRACLES, BUT FOR THE LOAVES.

In many cases religious differences are mainly verbal. There is an Eastern tale of four men, an Arab, a Persian, a Turk, and a Greek, who agreed to club together for an evening meal, but when they had done so they quarrelled as to what it should be. The Turk proposed Azum, the Arab Aneb, the Persian Anghur, while the Greek insisted on Stapylion. While they were disputing

> Before their eyes did pass,
> Laden with grapes, a gardener's ass.
> Sprang to his feet each man, and showed,
> With eager hand, that purple load.
> 'See Azum,' said the Turk; and 'see
> Anghur,' the Persian; 'what should be
> Better.' 'Nay Aneb, Aneb 'tis,'
> The Arab cried. The Greek said, 'This
> Is my Stapylion.' Then they bought
> Their grapes in peace.
> Hence be ye taught.

— Arnold

FAITH IS A **CHOICE**.

The very essence of faith is belief in a Supreme Being who delights in justice and mercy, whom all who would be saved are bound to obey, and whose worship consists in the practice of justice and charity toward our neighbors.

Faith is a knowledge within the heart, beyond the reach of proof.
— Khalil Gibran

Faith is not belief without proof, but trust without reservation.
— D. Elton Trueblood

FAITH BENEFITS HEALTH

Faith brings an increased sense of well-being, hope and optimism; lower rates of depression and suicide; less loneliness and less alcohol and drug abuse.

Those with religious involvement live longer—though no one knows whether longevity is due to their faith or their community ties.

FAITH CAUSES YOU TO KNOW IN YOUR HEART BEFORE YOU SEE WITH YOUR EYES.

"Seeing is believing." Once you see the thing hoped for already existing in the natural order, you don't need faith.

Faith is taking the first step even when you don't see the whole staircase.
— Martin Luther King, Jr.

To live in faith means to do and say what you believe is right, without doubting.

Faith consists in believing when it is beyond the power of reason to believe.
— Voltaire

Doubt is a pain too lonely to know that faith is his twin brother.
— Khalil Gibran

To have faith is to believe in something or someone, to fully trust, to be so confident that you base your actions on what you believe. To have faith is to be fully convinced of the truthfulness and reliability of that in which you believe.

A man of courage is also full of faith.
— Marcus Tullius Cicero

To profess an opinion for which you have no sufficient reason is clearly illogical, but when it is necessary to act you must do so on the best evidence available, however slight that may be.

RELIGION IS AN AFFAIR OF THE HEART AND NOT OF THE MIND ONLY.

Why should you expect Religion to solve questions with reference to the origin and destiny of the Universe? You do not expect the most elaborate treatise to tell you the origin of electricity or of heat. Natural History throws no light on the origin of life. Has Biology ever professed to explain existence?

The great Danish physicist Niels Bohr, it is said, had a good-luck horseshoe hanging in his office. "You don't believe in that nonsense, do you?" a visitor once asked, to which Bohr replied, "No, but they say it works whether you believe in it or not."

Faith is not contrary to reason.
— Sherwood Eddy

Nobel laureate physicist Steven Weinberg, an outspoken atheist, acknowledged that science is a poor substitute for the role religion plays in most peoples' lives.

Faith and prayer are the vitamins of the soul; man cannot live in health without them.
— Mahalia Jackson

It's hard to live in a world in which one's highest emotions can be understood in biochemical and evolutionary terms, rather than a gift from God. Instead of the big, comforting certainties promoted by religion, science can offer only "a lot of little truths.

> **In the midst of the sun is the light, in the midst of light is truth, and in the midst of truth is the imperishable being.**
> **— Vedas Saying**

Deity has been defined as a circle whose centre is everywhere, and whose circumference is nowhere.

We may be pardoned if we indulge ourselves in various speculations both as to our beginning and our end.

> **Our birth is but a sleep and a forgetting;**
> **The soul that rises with us, our life's star**
> **Hath had elsewhere its setting,**
> **And cometh from afar;**
> **Not in entire forgetfulness,**
> **And not in utter nakedness,**
> **But trailing clouds of glory do we come**
> **From God who is our home.**
> **— William Wordsworth**

Many have attempted to compound for wickedness in life by purity of belief, a vain and fruitless effort. To do right is the sure ladder that leads up to Heaven, though the true faith will help us to find and to climb it.

> **It is my duty to have loved the highest,**
> **It surely was my profit had I known,**
> **It would have been my pleasure had I**
> **seen.**
> — Alfred Lord Tennyson

Though religious truth can justify no bitterness, it is well worth any amount of thought and study.

> **Truth is the highest thing that**
> **man may keep.**
> — Chaucer

To arrive at truth spare yourself no pain, but certainly inflict none on others.

Quarrels will never advance religion, and that to persecute is no way to convert.

> **Do unto others as you would have others**
> **do unto you. This is the whole Law; the**
> **rest, merely Commentaries upon it.**
> — Hillel, the Elder

We are only just beginning to realize that a loving and merciful Father would not resent honest error, not even perhaps the attribution to him of such odious injustice.

> **The letter killeth, but the spirit giveth life.**
> — Jesus

If for every rebuke that we titter of men's vices, we put forth a claim upon their hearts; if, for every assertion of God's demands from them, we should substitute a display of His kindness to them; if side by side, with every warning of death, we could exhibit proofs and promises of immortality; if, in fine, instead of assuming the being of an awful Deity, which men, though they cannot and dare not deny, are always unwilling, sometimes unable, to conceive; we were to show them a near, visible, inevitable, out all-beneficent Deity, whose presence makes the earth itself a heaven, I think there would be fewer deaf children sitting in the market-place.

— John Ruskin

Whatever may be right about religion, to quarrel over it must be wrong.

Let others wrangle, I will wonder.
— St. Augustine

Those who suspend their judgment are not on that account sceptics, and it is often those who think they know most, who are especially troubled by doubts and anxiety.

Great God, I had rather be
A Pagan suckled in some creed outworn;
So might I, standing on this pleasant lea,
Have glimpses that would make me less forlorn.
— William Wordsworth

In religion, as with children at night, it is darkness and ignorance that create dread; light and love cast out fear.

FAITH AIDS IN THE TRANSITION TO THE OTHER SIDE.

Do not act as if thou wert going to live
ten thousand years.
Death hangs over thee.
While thou livest,
while it is in thy power, be good....

Since it is possible that thou mayest depart from life this very moment, regulate every act and thought accordingly. But to go away from among men, if there be gods, is not a thing to be afraid of, for the gods will not involve thee in evil; but if indeed they do not exist, or if they have no concern about human affairs, what is it to me to live in a universe devoid of gods, or devoid of Providence. But in truth they do exist, and they do care for human things, and they have put all the means in man's power to enable him not to fall into real evils. And as for the rest, if there was anything evil, they would have provided for this also, that it should be altogether in a man's power not to fall into it.

— Marcus Aurelius

Chapter 8

The Challenges in LIfe

*Life affords no higher pleasure than that
of surmounting difficulties, passing from
one step of success to another, forming
new wishes and seeing them gratified.*

— Samuel Johnson

L ife brings troubles of many kinds. Some
sorrows are real enough, especially
those you bring on yourself. Others are
mere ghosts of troubles, which, if you face
them boldly, you find that they have no
substance or reality, but are mere creations
of your morbid imagination.

**If you can find a path with no obstacles, it
probably doesn't lead anywhere.**
— Frank A. Clark

Some of your troubles are evils, but not
real; while others are real, but not evils.

**And yet, into how unfathomable a gulf
the mind rushes when the troubles of this
world agitate it. If it then forget its own
light, which is eternal joy, and rush into
the outer darkness, which are the cares**

of this world, as the mind now does, it knows nothing else but lamentations."
— Consolations of Boethius

OVERCOMING TROUBLES STRENGTHENS YOU.

Troubles are the barbells with which you exercise your skills.

If I had a formula for bypassing trouble, I would not pass it round. Trouble creates a capacity to handle it. I don't embrace trouble; that's as bad as treating it as an enemy. But I do say meet it as a friend, for you'll see a lot of it and had better be on speaking terms with it.
— Oliver Wendell Holmes

The way you think about events has much to do with the way you experience them.

If you don't like something change it; if you can't change it, change the way you think about it.
— Mary Engelbreit

HAPPINESS DEPENDS MORE ON WHAT IS WITHIN THAN WITHOUT.

Stone walls do not a prison make,
Nor iron bars a cage,
Minds innocent and quiet take
That for a hermitage.
"If I have freedom in my love,
And in my soul am free;
Angels alone that soar above
Enjoy such liberty.

— Lovelace.

Why then, 'tis none to you: for there is
nothing either good or bad, but thinking
makes it so: to me it is a prison.

— Rosencrantz

The greatest evils are from within us;
and from ourselves also we must look for
our greatest good.

— Jeremy Taylor

Milton in his blindness saw more beautiful visions, and Beethoven in his deafness heard more heavenly music, than most of us can ever hope to enjoy.

The mind is its own place, and in itself
Can make a Heaven of Hell,
a Hell of Heaven.

— John Milton

You are all apt to fear the worst when you know not what may happen.

WHEN YOU KNOW THE FULL EXTENT OF A DANGER, IT IS HALF OVER.

We dread ghosts more than robbers, not only without reason, but against reason; for even if ghosts existed, how could they hurt us? and in ghost stories, few, even those who say that they have seen a ghost, ever profess or pretend to have felt one.

I ask not for a lighter burden, but for broader shoulders.
— Jewish Proverb

We magnify troubles and difficulties, looking at them till they seem much greater than they really are.

Dangers are no more light, if they once seem light: and more dangers have deceived men than forced them: nay, it were better to meet some dangers half way, though they come nothing near, than to keep too long a watch upon their approaches: for if a man watch too long, it is odds he will fall asleep.
— Sir Francis Bacon

FORESIGHT IS VERY WISE,

BUT FORESORROW IS VERY FOOLISH.

Some of our troubles, no doubt, are real enough, but yet are not evils.

It often happens that by some false step, intentional or unintentional, you missed the right road, and went wrong. Can you then re-trace your steps? can you recover what is lost?

> **A word too much, or a kiss too long,**
> **And the world is never the same again.**

Selfishness is considered a fault.The pity is that so many people are foolishly selfish: that they pursue a course of action which neither makes themselves nor any one else happy.

> **Every man ought to begin with himself,**
> **and make his own happiness first, from**
> **which the happiness of the whole world**
> **would at last unquestionably follow.**
>
> **— Johann Wolfgang von Goethe**

It would be a great thing if people realized that they can never add to the sum of their happiness by doing wrong. In the case of children, indeed, we recognize this; we per-ceive that a spoilt child is not a happy one; that it would have been far better for him to have been punished at first and thus saved from greater suffering in after life.

Turn your wounds into wisdom.

— Oprah Winfrey

It is a beautiful idea that every man has with him a Guardian Angel; and it is true too: for Conscience is ever on the watch, ever ready to warn us of danger.

COMPLAINING IS MOST UNGRATEFUL.

For who would lose,
Though full of pain, this intellectual being,
Those thoughts that wander through Eternity;
To perish rather, swallowed up, and lost
In the wide womb of uncreated thought.

— John Milton

Some say you are sent here in preparation for another and a better world. If so, why complain of what is but a preparation for future happiness?

The problem is not that there are problems.
The problem is expecting otherwise and
thinking that having problems is a problem.

— Theodore Rubin

Sorrow

Count each affliction, whether light or grave,
God's messenger sent down to thee; do thou
With courtesy receive him; rise and bow
And ere his shadow pass thy threshold, crave
Permission first his heavenly feet to lave
Then lay before him all thou hast : Allow
No cloud of passion to usurp thy brow,
Or mar thy hospitality; no wave
Of mortal tumult to obliterate
The soul's marmoreal calmness: Grief should be,
Like joy, majestic, equable, sedate;
Confirming, cleansing, raising, making free;
Strong to consume small troubles; to commend
Great thoughts, grave thoughts,
thoughts lasting to the end.

— Aubrey De Vere

Grief shall be

Like joy, majestic, equable, sedate;
Confirming, cleansing, raising, making free;
Strong to consume small troubles; to commend
Great thoughts, grave thoughts, thoughts
lasting to the end.

— Aubrey de Vere

Life is awesome even in the darkests of days.

Does not a good man consider every day a feast?' ... Seeing then that life is the most complete initiation into all these things, it ought to be full of ease of mind and joy; and if properly understood, would enable us to acquiesce in the present without repining, to remember the past with thankfulness, and to meet the future hopefully and cheerfully without fear of suspicion.
— Plutarch

Who will tell whether one happy moment of love or the joy of breathing or walking on a bright morning and smelling the fresh air, is not worth all the suffering and effort which life implies.
— Erich Fromm

I have sometimes been wildly, despairingly, acutely miserable, but through it all I still know quite certainly that just to be alive is a grand thing.
— Agatha Christie

Chapter 10

The Gift of Laughter

*To read a good comedy is to keep the
best company in the world, when the best
things are said, and the most amusing
things happen.*

— William Hazlitt

Laughter appears to be the special pre-
rogative of man. The higher animals may
have reasoning power, but it is more than
doubtful whether they are capable of appre-
ciating a joke.

THERE IS A TIME TO LAUGH,
AS WELL AS TO WEEP.

The most wasted of all days is that on
which you have not laughed. It is no small
merit of laughter when it is spontaneous.

You cannot force people to laugh; you cannot give a reason why they should laugh;
they must laugh of themselves or not at
all.... If we think we must not laugh, this
makes our temptation to laugh the greater.

— William Hazlitt

Wit has solved many difficulties and decided many controversies.

> Ridicule shall frequently prevail,
> And cut the knot when graver reasons fail.
> — Francis

> Against the assault of laughter
> nothing can stand.
> — Mark Twain

LAUGHTER IS INFECTIOUS.

Laughter's sound is more contagious than coughs, sniffles, or sneezes.

> I am not only witty in myself, but the
> cause that wit is in other men.
> — Falstaff

Like port wine, some jokes may be better than others, but anything which makes one laugh is good.

> After all, it is a good thing to laugh at any
> rate; and if a straw can tickle a man, it is
> an instrument of happiness and of health.
> — Dryden

LAUGHTER IS THE BEST MEDICINE.

Not only is laughter fun, free, and easy to use, but it actually promotes healing. After Norman Cousins showed that laughing slowed the progression of cancer, laugh programs began appearing among protocols available in hospitals. Humor and laughter strengthen the immune system, boosts energy, diminishes pain, and reduces stress.

> **Hearty laughter is a good way to jog internally without having to go outdoors.**
> **— Norman Cousins**

Bring more laughter into your life.

> **A good time to laugh is any time you can.**
> **— Linda Ellerbee**

Associate with fun, playful people. Playful people laugh easily–at themselves and life's absurdities–and find the humor in everyday life.

> **A person who can bring the spirit of laughter into a room is indeed blessed.**
> **— Bennett Cerf**

We've all known the classic tight-jawed sourpuss who takes everything with deathly seriousness and never laughs at anything.

**Man, when you lose your laugh
you lose your footing.**
— **Ken Kesey**

Look at the lighter side of life.

Laughter is an instant vacation.
— **Milton Berle**

Humor takes you to a higher place where you can view the world from a more relaxed, positive, creative, joyful, and balanced perspective.

**I've always thought that a big laugh is a
really loud noise from the soul saying,
"Ain't that the truth".**
— **Quincy Jones**

Laughing helps you see things anew and to take yourself less seriously. It helps to put difficulties into perspective

A humorous perspective creates psychological distance, which can help you avoid feeling overwhelmed and frightened.

Comedy is defiance. It's a snort of contempt in the face of fear and anxiety. And it's the laughter that allows hope to creep back on the inhale.
— **Will Durst**

You can't feel anxious, angry, or sad when laughing. Laughing, especially deep belly laugh releases tension.

**Laughter is a tranquilizer
with no side effects.
— Arnold Glasow**

Laugh at yourself. Share embarrassing moments. Friends will love and laugh at themselves in you. And you release the parallelizing embarrassment.

**Every blessed one of you feels better for
that burst of laughter.
— Ivor Novello**

DON'T BEMOAN SITUATIONS;
LAUGH AT THEM.

Look for the irony and absurdity of life.

**A man isn't poor if he can still laugh.
— Raymond Hitchcock**

**What soap is to the body,
laughter is to the soul.
— Yiddish Proverb**

Shared laughter binds us together, increasing happiness and intimacy. Laughing with a friend strengthens bonds, providing a buffer against stress, disagreements, and disappointment.

Laughter is the shortest distance between two people.
— Victor Borge

Smile. When you smile, the world smiles back. Smiling contributes to world peace. When you see something even mildly pleasing, practice smiling.

When people are laughing, they're generally not killing each other.
— Alan Alda

I believe that laughter is a language of God and that we can all live happily ever laughter.
— Yakov Smirnoff

The ability to laugh, play, and have fun with others not only makes life more enjoyable–it also helps you solve problems, connect with others, and be more creative.

Remember, men need laughter sometimes more than food.
— Anna Fellows Johnston

Time spent laughing is time
spent with the gods.
— Japanese proverb

Chapter 11

The Spur of Ambition

Fame is the spur that the clear spirit doth raise
That last infirmity of noble minds
To scorn delights and live laborious days.

— John Milton

Striving to achieve, to stretch, to accomplish and do better than peers is the spur that motivates laborious days.

It is not the critic who counts; not the man who points out how the strong man stumbles, or where the doer of deeds could have done them better. The credit belongs to the man who is actually in the arena, whose face is marred by dust and sweat and blood, who strives valiantly; who errs and comes short again and again; because there is not effort without error and shortcomings; but who does actually strive to do the deed; who knows the great enthusiasm, the great devotion, who spends himself in a worthy cause, who at the best knows in the end the triumph of high achievement and who at the worst, if he fails, at least he fails while daring greatly.
                                      - Theodore Roosevelt

ALL SUCCEED WHO DESERVE, THOUGH NOT PERHAPS AS THEY HOPED.

I learned this, at least, by my experiment;
that if one advances confidently in the
direction of his dreams, and endeavors to
live the life which he has imagined, he will
meet with a success unexpected in common hours. He will put some things behind, will pass an invisible boundary; new,
universal, and more liberal laws will begin
to establish themselves around and within
him; or the old laws be expanded, and
interpreted in his favor in a more liberal
sense, and he will live with the license of a
higher order of beings. In proportion as he
simplifies his life, the laws of the universe
will appear less complex, and solitude
will not be solitude, nor poverty poverty,
nor weakness weakness. If you have built
castles in the air, your work need not be
lost: that is where they should be. Now
put the foundations under them.
— Henry David Thoreau

An honorable defeat is better than a mean
victory, and no one is really the worse
for being beaten, unless you lose heart.
Though you may not be able to attain, that
is no reason why you should not aspire.

**If a man look sharp and attentively he
shall see fortune; for though she is blind,
she is not invisible.**

— Sir Francis Bacon

Ambition is the drive that sparks you—enlivening. Without it, there is little on the horizon to draw you forward.

**A young man without ambition is an old
man waiting to be.**

— Steven Brust

For a reasonable prospect of success you must first realize what you hope to achieve; and then make the most of your opportunities.

USE OF TIME IS MOST IMPORTANT.

**Without ambition one starts nothing.
Without work one finishes nothing. The
prize will not be sent to you. You have
to win it. The man who knows how will
always have a job. The man who also
knows why will always be his boss.**

- Ralph Waldo Emerson

When the mind is made up, there must be no looking back. Spare yourself no labor, nor shrink from any challenge.

He either fears his fate too much
Or his deserts are small,
That dares not put it to the touch
To gain or lose it all.
— Montros

Ambition can creep as well as soar.
— Edmund Burke

What is glory?

A spider is proud when it has caught a fly,
a man when he has caught a hare, another
when he has taken a little fish in a net,
another when he has taken wild boars,
another when he has taken bears, and another when he has taken Sarmatians:
— Marcus Aurelius

The vanity of fame encourages with the evidence that anyone may succeed if their objects are but reasonable.

Ambition is so powerful a passion in the
human breast, that however high we
reach we are never satisfied.
— Niccolò Machiavelli

Man exists for culture; not for what
he can accomplish, but for what can be
accomplished in him.
— Ralph Waldo Emerson

TO BE REMEMBERED IS NOT NECESSARILY TO BE FAMOUS.

There is infamy as well as fame; and unhappily almost as many are remembered for the one as for the other, and not a few for the mixture of both.

> To be nameless in worthy deeds exceeds an infamous history. The Canaanitish woman lives more happily without a name than Herodias with one; and who would not rather have been the good thief than Pilate?
>
> — Sir J. Browne

Kings and Generals are often remembered as much for their deaths as for their lives, for their misfortunes as for their successes.

> The general who advances without coveting fame and retreats without fearing disgrace, whose only thought is to protect his country and do good service for his sovereign, is the jewel of the kingdom.
>
> — Sun Tzu

A surer and more glorious title to fame is that of those who are remembered for some act of justice or self-devotion, like Goethe who has been called "the soul of his century".

Statesmen and Generals enjoy great celebrity during their lives. But the fame of the Philosopher and Poet is more enduring.

THE REAL CONQUERORS OF THE WORLD ARE THE THINKERS, NOT THE WARRIORS.

Not Genghis Khan and Akbar, Rameses, or Alexander, but Confucius and Buddha, Aristotle, Plato, and Christ. Such men's lives cannot be compressed into any biography. They lived not merely in their own generation, but for all time.

When we speak of the Elizabethan period we think of Shakespeare and Bacon, Raleigh and Spenser. The ministers and secretaries of state, with one or two exceptions, we scarcely remember, and Bacon himself is recollected less as the Judge than as the Philosopher.

To what do Generals and Statesmen owe their fame? They were celebrated for their deeds, but to the Poet and the Historian they owe their fame, and to the Poet and Historian we owe their glorious memories and the example of their virtues.

My dear and only love. I'll make thee glorious by my pen and famous by my sword.
— Montrose

It is remarkable, and encouraging, how many of the greatest men have risen from the lowest rank, and triumphed over obstacles that seemed insurmountable; nay, even obscurity itself may be a source of honor.

It is, on the other hand, sad to think how many of our greatest benefactors are unknown even by name. Who discovered the art of procuring fire? Prometheus is merely the personification of forethought. Who invented letters? Cadmus is a mere name.

Great men, unknown to their generation, have their fame among the great who have preceded them, and all true worldly fame subsides from their high estimate beyond the stars.
— Henry David Thoreau

These inventions, indeed, are lost in the mists of antiquity, but even as regards recent progress the steps are often so gradual, and so numerous, that few inventions can be attributed entirely, or even mainly, to any one person.

Chapter 12

The Benefits of Wealth

*The rich and poor meet together: the Lord
is the maker of them all.*

— Proverbs of Solomon

Money and the love of money often go
together. The poor man, as Emerson
says, is the man who wishes to be rich; and
the more a man has, the more he often longs
to be richer. Just as drinking often does but
increase thirst; so in many cases the craving
for riches does grow with wealth.

It is often easier to make money
than to keep or to enjoy it.

Keeping money is a dull and anxious
drudgery. Money's value depends partly on
knowing what to do with it, partly on the
manner in which it is acquired.

**Acquire money, thy friends say, that
we also may have some. If I can acquire
money and also keep myself modest, and
faithful, and magnanimous, point out the
way, and I will acquire it. But if you ask**

me to love the things which are good
and my own, in order that you may gain
things that are not good, see how unfair
and unwise you are. For which would you
rather have? Money, or a faithful and
modest friend....
— Epictetus

Midas prayed that everything he touched
might be turned into gold, and this prayer
was granted. His wine turned to gold, his
bread turned to gold, his clothes, his very
bed. He suffered from too much gold.

**Whether wealth is an advantage
depends on the use you make of it.**

Knowledge and Strength, Beauty and Skill,
may all be abused; if we neglect or misuse
them we are worse off than if we had never
had them.

Wealth brings command of leisure, the
power of helping friends, books, works of
art, opportunities of all kinds, and means of
travel—and much more.

Money is well worth having, and worth
working for, so long as it does not require
too great a sacrifice.

Gold may be bought too dear.
— Wise Proverb

If wealth is to be valued because it gives leisure, clearly it would be a mistake to sacrifice leisure in the struggle for wealth.

Money has a tendency to make men poor in spirit. Yet, what is there that is without danger?

> I desire money," he said, "because I think I know the use of it. It commands labor, it gives leisure; and to give leisure to those who will employ it in the forwarding of truth is the noblest present an individual can make to the whole.
> **— Shelley**

> Abroad with my wife, the first time that ever I rode in my own coach; which do make my heart rejoice and praise God, and pray him to bless it to me, and continue it.
> **— Pepys**

If life has been sacrificed to the rolling up of money for its own sake, the very means by which it was acquired will prevent its being enjoyed.

For Misers, the chill of poverty has entered into their very bones. They are miser-able.

> A collector peeps into all the picture shops of Europe for a landscape of Poussin, a crayon sketch of Salvator; but the Transfiguration, the Last Judgment, the Communion of St. Jerome, and what are as transcendent as these, are on the walls of the Vatican, the Uffizi, or the Louvre, where every footman may see them: to say nothing of Nature's pictures in every street, of sunsets and sunrises every day, and the sculpture of the human body never absent. A collector recently bought at public auction in London, for one hundred and fifty-seven guineas, an autograph of Shakespeare: but for nothing a schoolboy can read Hamlet, and can detect secrets of highest concernment yet unpublished therein.
>
> — Ralph Waldo Emerson

> What hath the owner but the sight of it with his eyes.
>
> — Solomo

You are really richer than you think. People envy a great Landlord, and fancy how delightful it must be to possess a large estate.

If you own land, the land owns you.
— Ralph Waldo Emerson

The commons, and roads, and footpaths, and the seashore, our grand and varied coast—these are all ours—yours!

WE ARE ALL GREAT LAND PROPRIETORS,
IF WE ONLY KNEW IT.

What we lack is not land, but the power to enjoy it. Moreover, this great inheritance has the additional advantage that it entails no labor, requires no management.

THE LANDLORD HAS THE TROUBLE,
BUT THE LANDSCAPE BELONGS TO
ANY ONE WITH EYES TO SEE IT.

Chapter 13

A Song of Books

Oh for a booke and a shadie nooke,
Eyther in doore or out;
With the grene leaves whispering overhead
Or the streete cryes all about.
Where I maie reade all at my ease,
Both of the newe and old;
For a jollie goode booke whereon to looke,
Is better to me than golde.

— Old English Song

Of all the privileges we enjoy there is none for which we ought to be more thankful than for books.

Books are the masters who instruct us without rods and rules, without hard words and anger, without clothes or money. If you approach them, they are not asleep; if investigating you interrogate them, they conceal nothing; if you mistake them, they never grumble; if you are ignorant, they cannot laugh at you. The library, therefore, of wisdom is more precious than all riches, and nothing that can be wished for is worthy to be compared with it.

— Richard de Bury, Bishop of Durham

Books are real friends.

Outside of a dog, a book is man's best friend. Inside of a dog it's too dark to read.

— Groucho Marx

You know you've read a good book when you turn the last page and feel a little as if you have lost a friend.

— Paul Sweeney

Books are the quietest and most constant of friends; they are the most accessible and wisest of counselors, and the most patient of teachers.

— Charles William Elliot

There is no friend as loyal as a book.

— Ernest Hemingway

He that loveth a book will never want a faithful friend, a wholesome counselor, a cheerful companion, an effectual comforter.

— Isaac Barrow

Books are a guide in youth and an entertainment for age. They support us under solitude, and keep us from being a burthen to ourselves. They help us to forget the crossness of men and things; compose our cares and our passions; and lay our disappointments asleep.

— Jeremy Collier

Books bring a university into your home.

A collection of books is a real university.

— Carlyle

My alma mater was books, a good library.... I could spend the rest of my life reading, just satisfying my curiosity.

— Malcolm X

Books are a necessity for a full life.

A room without books is like a body without a soul.

— Marcus Tullius Cicero

If you have a garden and a library, you have everything you need.

— Marcus Tullius Cicero

A Studious Boy Lingering
at a Bookstall

I saw a boy with eager eye
Open a book upon a stall,
And read, as he'd devour it all;
Which, when the stall man did espy,
Soon to the boy I heard him call,
'You, sir, you never buy a book,
Therefore in one you shall not look.'
The boy passed slowly on, and with a sigh
He wished he never had been taught to read,
Then of the old churl's books he should have
had no need.

— Mary Lamb

The variety of books is endless.

A library contains infinite riches
in a little room.

— Marlowe

You may sit at home with a book and yet be
in all quarters of the earth. You may travel
round the world with Captain Cook or Dar-
win, with Kingsley or Ruskin, who will show
you much more perhaps than ever you
should see for yourself.

A great book should leave you with many experiences, and slightly exhausted at the end. You live several lives while reading.

— William Styron

The world itself has no limits when you have books. Humboldt and Herschel will carry you far away to the mysterious nebulae, beyond the sun and even the stars: time has no more bounds than space; history stretches out behind us, and geology will carry you back for millions of years before the creation of man, even to the origin of the material Universe itself. Nor are you limited to one plane of thought. Aristotle and Plato will transport you into a new sphere.

Comfort and consolation, refreshment and happiness, may indeed be found in his library by any one "who shall bring the golden key that unlocks its silent door".

— Matthews

A library is true fairyland, a very palace of delight, a haven of repose from the storms and troubles of the world.

Books may well be the only true magic.

— Alice Hoffman

Rich and poor can enjoy books equally, for within their pages wealth gives no advantage.

A library is a true paradise on earth, a garden of Eden without its one drawback; for all is open to us, including, and especially, the fruit of the Tree of Knowledge, for which we are told that our first mother sacrificed all the Pleasures of Paradise.

We may read the most important histories, the most exciting volumes of travels and adventures, the most interesting stories, the most beautiful poems; we may meet the most eminent statesmen, poets, and philosophers, benefit by the ideas of the greatest thinkers, and enjoy the grandest creations of human genius.

Books are the plane, and the train, and the road. They are the destination, and the journey. They are home.

— Anna Quindlen

It is one thing to own a library; it is quite another to use it wisely.

If you only read the books that everyone else is reading, you can only think what everyone else is thinking.

— Haruki Murakami

Some would burn books

And on the subject of burning books: I want to congratulate librarians, not famous for their physical strength or their powerful political connections or their great wealth, who, all over this country, have staunchly resisted anti-democratic bullies who have tried to remove certain books from their shelves, and have refused to reveal to thought police the names of persons who have checked out those titles.

The America I love still exists at the front desks of our public libraries.

— Kurt Vonnegut

Chapter 14

The Power of Art

*Art (caeteris paribus) is great in exact
proportion to the love of beauty shown by
the painter, provided that love of beauty
forfeit no atom of truth.*

— John Ruskin

Art is unquestionably one of the purest
and highest elements in human happiness. It trains the mind through the eye,
and the eye through the mind. As the sun
colors flowers, so does art color life.

**In true Art, the hand, the head, and the
head of man go together. But Art is no
recreation: it cannot be learned at spare
moments, nor pursued when we have
nothing better to do.**

— John Ruskin

Study and labor cannot make every man an
artist, but no one can succeed in art without them. In Art two and two do not make
four, and no number of little things will
make a great one.

It has been said, and on high authority, that the end of art is to please. But this is a very imperfect definition. It might as well be said that a library is only intended for pleasure and ornament.

Poets tell us that Prometheus, having made a beautiful statue of Minerva, the goddess was so delighted that she offered to bring down anything from Heaven which could add to its perfection. Prometheus on this prudently asked her to take him there, so that he might choose for himself. This Minerva did, and Prometheus, finding that in heaven all things were animated by fire, brought back a spark, with which he gave life to his work.

IMITATION IS THE MEANS AND NOT THE END OF ART.

To imitate the *Iliad*, says Dr. Young, is not imitating Homer, but as Sir J. Reynolds adds, the more the artist studies nature "the nearer he approaches to the true and perfect idea of art."

Following these rules and using these precautions, when you have clearly and distinctly learned in what good coloring

consists, you cannot do better than have recourse to Nature herself, who is always at hand, and in comparison of whose true splendor the best colored pictures are but faint and feeble.

— Sir J.Reynolds

ART MUST CREATE AS WELL AS COPY.

The ideal without the real lacks life; but the real without the ideal lacks pure beauty. Both need to unite; to join hands and enter into alliance. In this way the best work may be achieved. Thus beauty is an absolute idea, and not a mere copy of imperfect Nature.

— Victor Cousin

Remember that so far as the eye is concerned, the object of the artist is to train, not to deceive, and that his higher function has reference rather to the mind than to the eye.

To gild refined gold, to paint the lily,
To throw a perfume on the violet,
To smooth the ice, or add another hue
Unto the rainbow, or with taper-light
To seek the beauteous eye of heaven to garnish,
Is wasteful and ridiculous excess.

— Shakespeare

All is not gold that glitters, flowers are not all arrayed like the lily, and there is room for selection as well as representation.

> The true, the good, and the beautiful, are but forms of the infinite: what then do we really love in truth, beauty, and virtue? We love the infinite himself. The love of the infinite substance is hidden under the love of its forms. It is so truly the infinite which charms in the true, the good, and the beautiful, that its manifestations alone do not suffice. The artist is dissatisfied at the sight even of his greatest works; he aspires still higher.
>
> — Cousin

It is sometimes objected that Landscape painting is not true to nature; but we must ask, What is truth? Is the object to produce the same impression on the mind as that created by the scene itself? If so, let any one try to draw from memory a group of mountains, and he will probably find that in the impression produced on his mind the mountains are loftier and steeper, the valleys deeper and narrower, than in the actual reality.

> Art is called Art simply because it is not Nature.
> — Johann Wolfgang von Goethe

Artists must not be mere copyists. Something higher and more subtle is required. They must create, or at any rate interpret, as well as copy.

Caracci said that poets paint in their words and artists speak in their works. The latter have indeed one great advantage, for a glance at a statue or a painting will convey a more vivid idea than a long and minute description.

ART IS UNDERSTOOD
BY ALL CIVILIZED NATIONS,
WHILST EACH HAS A SEPARATE LANGUAGE.

The mission of Art is like that of woman. It is not Hers so much to do the hard toil and moil of the world, as to surround it with a halo of beauty, to convert work into pleasure.

Science and Art are sisters, or rather perhaps they are like brother and sister.

It has been the happy combination of art and science which has trained us to perceive the beauty which surrounds us.

Art helps us to see

Hundreds of people can talk for one who can think; but thousands can think for one who can see. To see clearly is poetry, prophecy, and religion all in one.... Remembering always that there are two characters in which all greatness of Art consists—first, the earnest and intense seizing of natural facts; then the ordering those facts by strength of human intellect, so as to make them, for all who look upon them, to the utmost serviceable, memorable, and beautiful. And thus great Art is nothing else than the type of strong and noble life; for as the ignoble person, in his dealings with all that occurs in the world about him, first sees nothing clearly, looks nothing fairly in the face, and then allows himself to be swept away by the trampling torrent and unescapable force of the things that he would not foresee and could not understand: so the noble person, looking the facts of the world full in the face, and fathoming them with deep faculty, then deals with them in unalarmed intelligence and unhurried strength, and becomes, with his human intellect and will, no unconscious nor insignificant agent in consummating their good and restraining their evil.

— John Ruskin

Poetry is an art divine.

> Though the arts are in some respects
> isolated, yet there is one which seems to
> profit by the resources of all, and that
> is Poetry. With words, Poetry can paint
> and sculpture; she can build edifices like
> an architect; she unites, to some extent,
> melody and music. She is, so to say, the
> center in which all arts unite.
>
> — Cousin

A true poem is a gallery of pictures.

> It must, I think, be admitted that painting
> and sculpture can give us a clearer and
> more vivid idea of an object we have nev-
> er seen than any description can convey.
> But when we have once seen it, then on
> the contrary there are many points which
> the poet brings before us, and which
> perhaps neither in the representation,
> nor even in nature, should we perceive
> for ourselves. Objects can be most vividly
> brought before us by the artist, actions
> by the poet; space is the domain of Art,
> time of Poetry.
>
> — Lessing's Laocoön

Great poets must be inspired; they must possess an exquisite sense of beauty, and feelings deeper than those of most people, and yet well under their control.

> **The Milton of poetry is the man, in his own magnificent phrase, of devout prayer to that eternal spirit that can enrich with all utterance and knowledge, and sends out his seraphim with the hallowed fire of his altar, to touch and purify the lips of whom he pleases.**
>
> **— Arnold**

If from one point of view Poetry brings home to us the immeasurable inequalities of different minds, on the other hand it teaches us that genius is no affair of rank or wealth.

> **I think of Chatterton, the marvellous boy,**
> **The sleepless soul, that perish'd in his pride;**
> **Of Burns, that walk'd in glory and in joy**
> **Behind his plough upon the mountain-side.**
>
> **— Coleridge**

Second-rate poets fade gradually into dreamland; but the great poets remain always. Poetry will not live unless it be alive,

> **That which comes from the head**
> **goes to the heart.**
>
> **— William Wordsworth**

For he who, having no touch of the Muses' madness in his soul, comes to the door and thinks he will get into the temple by the help of Art—he, I say, and his Poetry are not admitted.

— Plato

THE WORK OF THE TRUE POET IS IMMORTAL.

For have not the verses of Homer continued 2500 years or more without the loss of a syllable or a letter, during which time infinite palaces, temples, castles, cities, have been decayed and demolished?

— Sir Francis Bacon

Poetry is the fruit of genius. Some wonder if Poetry is of any use, just as if to give pleasure were not useful in itself.

We must not estimate the works of genius merely with reference to the pleasure they afford, even when pleasure was their principal object. We must also regard the intelligence which they presuppose and exercise.

— St. Hailare

Thoroughly to enjoy Poetry we must not so limit ourselves, but must rise to a higher ideal.

Yes; constantly in reading poetry, a sense for the best, the really excellent, and of the strength and joy to be drawn from it, should be present in our minds, and should govern our estimate of what we read.
— Arnold

The Hebrews well-called their poets "Seers," for they not only perceive more than others, but also help other men to see much which would otherwise be lost to us. The old Greek word was [Greek: *aoidos*]—the Bard or Singer.

Poetry lifts the veil from the beauty of the world which would otherwise be hidden, and throws over the most familiar objects the glow and halo of imagination. The man who has a love for Poetry can scarcely fail to derive intense pleasure from Nature, which to those who love it is all "beauty to the eye and music to the ear."

> Yet Nature never set forth the earth in so
> rich tapestry as divers poets have done;
> neither with so pleasant rivers, fruit-
> ful trees, sweet-smelling flowers, nor
> whatsoever else may make the too-much-
> loved earth more lovely.
>
> — Sydney

In the smokiest city the poet will transport you, as if by enchantment, to the fresh air and bright sun, to the murmur of woods and leaves and water, to the ripple of waves upon sand, and enable you, as in some delightful dream, to cast off the cares and troubles of life.

The poet, indeed, must have more true knowledge, not only of human nature, but of all Nature, than other men are gifted with.

> Call it not vain; they do not err
> Who say that, when the poet dies,
> Mute Nature mourns her worshipper,
> And celebrates his obsequies.
>
> — Scott

To appreciate Poetry we must not merely glance at it, or rush through it, or read it in order to talk or write about it. You must compose yourself into the right frame of mind.

Poetry lengthens life; it creates time, if time be realized as the succession of ideas and not of minutes; it is the "breath and finer spirit of all knowledge;" it is bound neither by time nor space, but lives in the spirit of man. What greater praise can be given than the saying that life should be Poetry put into action.

Chapter 15

The Mystery of Music

Music is a moral law. It gives a soul to the universe, wings to the mind, flight to the imagination, a charm to sadness, gaiety and life to everything. It is the essence of order, and leads to all that is good, just, and beautiful, of which it is the invisible, but nevertheless dazzling, passionate, and eternal form.

— Plato

Voice has been a source of melody from the commencement of human existence. Probably percussion came first, then wind instruments, and lastly, those with strings: first the Drum, then the Flute, and thirdly, the Lyre.

The contest between Marsyas and Apollo is supposed to typify the struggle between the Flute and the Lyre; Marsyas representing the archaic Flute, Apollo the champion of the Lyre. The latter of course was victorious: it sets the voice free, and the sound

**Of music that is born of human breath
Comes straighter to the soul than any strain
The hand alone can make.**
— Morris

MYTHS HAVE EVOLVED TO EXPLAIN THE ORIGIN OF MUSIC.

One Greek tradition was to the effect Grasshoppers were human beings themselves in a world before the Muses; that when the Muses came, being ravished with delight, they sang and sang and forgot to eat, until

they died of hunger for the love of song. And they carry to heaven the report of those who honor them on earth.

— Plato

Authors of some of the loveliest music are unknown to us. This is the case for instance with the exquisite song "Drink to me only with thine eyes," the words of which were taken by Jonson from Philostratus, and which has been considered as the most beautiful of all "people's songs."

Music is capable of giving intense pleasure. To the sportsman, what Music can excel that of the hounds themselves? The cawing of rooks has been often quoted as a sound which has no actual beauty of its own, and yet which is delightful from its associations.

There is a true Music of Nature—the song of birds, the whisper of leaves, the ripple of waters upon a sandy shore, the wail of wind or sea.

Music seems as if it scarcely belonges to this material universe, but is

> **A tone of some world far from ours,**
> **Where music, and moonlight, and feeling are one.**
> **— Swinburne**

Music is in speech as well as in song. Not merely in the voice of those we love, and the charm of association, but in actual melody.

> **The Angel ended, and in Adam's ear**
> **So charming left his voice, that he awhile**
> **Thought him still speaking, still stood fixed to hear.**
> **— John Milton**

It is remarkable that more pains are not taken with the voice in conversation as well as in singing, for

> **What plea so tainted and corrupt**
> **But, being seasoned with a gracious voice,**
> **Obscures the show of evil.**
> **— John Milton**

Those who do not appreciate music have no heart.

> The man that hath no Music in himself
> Nor is not moved with concord of sweet sounds
> Is fit for treasons, stratagems, and spoils;
> — Shakespeare

Poets have sung most sweetly in praise of song. Milton invokes music as a luxury.

> And ever against eating cares
> Lap me in soft Lydian airs;
> Married to immortal verse
> Such as the meeting soul may pierce,
> In notes with many a winding bout
> Of linked sweetness long drawn out;
> With wanton heed, and giddy cunning,
> The melting voice through mazes running;
> Untwisting all the chains that tie
> The hidden soul of harmony.
> — John Milton

Sometimes music is a temptation.

> And she, more sweet than any bird on bough
> Would oftentimes amongst them bear a part,
> And strive to passe (as she could well enough)
> Their native musicke by her skilful art.

Or as an element of pure happiness—

There is in Souls a sympathy with sounds;
And as the mind is pitched, the ear is pleased
With melting airs or martial, brisk or grave;
Some chord in unison with what we hear
Is touched within us, and the heart replies.
How soft the music of those village bells,
Falling at intervals upon the ear
In cadence sweet, now dying all away,
Now pealing loud again and louder still
Clear and sonorous, as the gale comes on.
— Cowper

Music touches the human heart.

The soul of music slumbers in the shell,
Till waked and kindled by the master's spell,
And feeling hearts—touch them but lightly—pour
A thousand melodies unheard before.
— Rogers

Music enhances relgious worship.

As from the power of sacred lays
The spheres began to move,
And sung the great Creator's praise
To all the blessed above,
So when the last and dreadful hour
This crumbling pageant shall devour,
The trumpet shall be heard on high.
The dead shall live, the living die,
And music shall untune the sky.
— Dryden

Poets have always attributed to Music a power even over the inanimate forces of Nature.

> The rude sea grew civil at her song,
> And certain stars shot madly from their spheres
> To hear the Sea-maid's music.
> — Shakespeare

Prose writers have been inspired by Music to their highest eloquence.

> Music is a moral law. It gives a soul to the universe, wings to the mind, flight to the imagination, a charm to sadness, gaiety and life to everything. It is the essence of order, and leads to all that is good, just, and beautiful, of which it is the invisible, but nevertheless dazzling, passionate, and eternal form.
> — Plato

> Music is a fair and glorious gift from God. I would not for the world renounce my humble share in music.
> — Luther

> Music is an art that God has given us, in which the voices of all nations may unite their prayers in one harmonious rhythm.
> — Halevy

Music is a kind of inarticulate, unfathomable speech, which leads us to the edge
of the infinite, and lets us for moments
gaze into it.

— Carlyle

Song is a sweet companion of labor. The
rude chant of the boatman floats upon the
water, the shepherd sings upon the hill, the
milkmaid in the dairy, the ploughman at
the plough. Every trade, every occupation,
every act and scene of life, has long had its
own especial music. The bride went to her
marriage, the laborer to his work, the old
man to his last long rest, each with appro-
priate and immemorial music.

Music is the mother of sympathy, the hand-
maid of Religion, and will never exercise
its full effect unless it aims not merely to
charm the ear, but to touch the heart.

MUSIC IS A JOY FOR ALL.

Good Music does not necessarily involve
any considerable outlay; it is even now no
mere luxury of the rich, and we may hope
that as time goes on, it will become more
and more the comfort and solace of the
poor.

Chapter 16

The Beauty of Nature

Speak to the earth and it shall teach thee.

— Job

Any sketch of the blessings of life must contain special reference to this lovely world that the Greeks happily called *chosmosm* or beauty

God saw every thing that he had made, and, behold, it was very good.

— Genesis

How few of us appreciate the beautiful world in which we live! We walk through the world like ghosts, as if we were in it, but not of it. We have "eyes and see not, ears and hear not."

TO LOOK IS MUCH LESS EASY THAN TO OVERLOOK, AND TO BE ABLE TO SEE WHAT WE DO SEE, IS A GREAT GIFT.

The greatest thing a human soul ever does in this world is to see something, and tell what it saw in a plain way.

— John Ruskin

WE MUST LOOK BEFORE
WE CAN EXPECT TO SEE.

To the attentive eye, each moment of the
year has its own beauty; and in the same
field it beholds every hour a picture that
was never seen before, and shall never
be seen again. The heavens change every
moment and reflect their glory or gloom
on the plains beneath.
— Ralph Waldo Emerson

Love of Nature is a great gift. Nature indeed
provides without stint the main requisites
of human happiness.

To watch the corn grow, or the blossoms set;
to draw hard breath over plough-share or
spade; to read, to think, to love, to pray are
the things that make men happy.
— John Ruskin

When a man has such things to think on,
and sees the sun, the moon, and stars,
and enjoys earth and sea, he is not soli-
tary or even helpless.
— Epictetus

LIFE IS LUXURY FILLED WITH EXQUISITE BEAUTY.

Early summer has a special charm. The air is full of scent, and sound, and sunshine, of the song of birds and the murmur of insects; the meadows gleam with golden buttercups, it almost seems as if we could see the grass grow and the buds open; the bees hum for very joy, and the air is full of a thousand scents, above all perhaps that of new-mown hay.

Pageant of Summer

I linger in the midst of the long grass, the luxury of the leaves, and the song in the very air. I seem as if I could feel all the glowing life the sunshine gives and the south wind calls to being. The endless grass, the endless leaves, the immense strength of the oak expanding, the unalloyed joy of finch and blackbird; from all of them I receive a little.... In the blackbird's melody one note is mine; in the dance of the leaf shadows the formed maze is for me, though the motion is theirs; the flowers with a thousand faces have collected the kisses of the morning. Feeling with them, I receive some, at least, of their fulness of life. Never could

I have enough; never stay long enough....
The hours when the mind is absorbed by
beauty are the only hours when we really live, so that the longer we can stay
among these things so much the more is
snatched from inevitable Time.... These
are the only hours that are not wasted-
these hours that absorb the soul and fill
it with beauty. This is real life, and all
else is illusion, or mere endurance. To be
beautiful and to be calm, without mental
fear, is the ideal of Nature. If I cannot
achieve it, at least I can think it."
— Jefferies

Each season has its own special charm.

The daughters of the year
Dance into light and die into the shade.
— Alfred Lord Tennyson

THE RICHNESS OF LIFE IS WONDERFUL.

Any one who sits quietly on the grass and
watch a little will be indeed surprised at the
number and variety of living beings, every one
with a special history of its own, every one of-
fering endless problems of great interest.

If indeed thy heart were right, then would
every creature be to thee a mirror of
lifer and a book of holy doctrine.
— Thomas à Kempis.

Towns are beautiful, too. They teem with
human interest and historical associations.

Earth has not anything to show more fair;
Dull would he be of soul who could pass by
A sight so touching in its majesty:
This City now doth, like a garment, wear
The beauty of the morning; silent, bare,
Ships, towers, domes, theatres, and temples lie
Open unto the fields, and to the sky;
All bright and glittering in the smokeless air.
Never did sun more beautifully steep
In his first splendor, valley, rock, or hill;
Ne'er saw I, never felt, a calm so deep!
The river glideth at its own sweet will:
Dear God! the very houses seem asleep;
And all that mighty heart is lying still!"

— William Wordsworth

After a time in a great city, one feels a long-
ing for the country.

The meanest floweret of the vale,
The simplest note that swells the gale,
The common sun, the air, the skies,
To him are opening paradise.

— Gray

When in any great town we think of the country, flowers seem first to suggest themselves.

> Flowers seem intended for the solace of ordinary humanity. Children love them; quiet, tender, contented, ordinary people love them as they grow; luxurious and disorderly people rejoice in them gathered. They are the cottager's treasure; and in the crowded town mark, as with a little broken fragment of rainbow the windows of the workers in whose heart rest the covenant of peace.
> — John Ruskin,

In the crowded street flowers always seem as if they were pining for the freedom of the woods and fields, where they can live and grow as they please.

There are flowers for all seasons and all places. Flowers for spring, summer, and autumn—even in the depth of winter. There are flowers of the fields and woods and hedgerows, of the seashore and the lake's margin, of the mountain-side up to the very edge of the eternal snow.

Daffodils

That come before the swallow dares, and take
The winds of March with beauty; violets, dim,
But sweeter than the lids of Juno's eyes,
Or Cytherea's breath; pale primroses,
That die unmarried, ere they can behold
Bright Phoebus in his strength, a malady
Most incident to maids; bold oxlips and
The crown imperial; lilies of all kinds,
The flower-de-luce being one.

— Shakespeare

Daffodils are not mere delights to the eye; they are full of mystery and suggestions. They almost seem like enchanted princesses waiting for some princely deliverer.

To me the meanest flower that blows can give
Thoughts that do often lie too deep for tears.
— William Wordsworth

Every color, every variety of form, has some purpose and explanation.

LEAVES ADD EVEN MORE TO THE BEAUTY OF NATURE.

Every tree is a picture in itself: The gnarled and rugged Oak, the symbol and source of our navy, sacred to the memory of the Druids, the type of strength, the sovereign of British trees; the Chestnut, with its beautiful, tapering, and rich green, glossy leaves, its delicious fruit, and to the durability of which we owe the grand and historic roof of Westminster Abbey.

The Birch is the queen of trees, with her feathery foliage, scarcely visible in spring but turning to leaves of gold in autumn; the pendulous twigs tinged with purple, and silver stems so brilliantly marked with black and white.

The Elm forms grand masses of foliage which turn a beautiful golden yellow in autumn; and the Black Poplar with its perpendicular leaves, rustling and trembling with every breath of wind, towers over most other forest trees.

The Beech enlivens the country by its tender green in spring, rich green in summer, and glorious gold and orange in autumn, set off by the graceful gray stems; and has moreover, such a wealth of leaves that in autumn there are enough not only to clothe the tree itself but to cover the grass underneath.

If the Beech owes much to its delicate gray stem, even more beautiful is the reddish crimson of the Scotch Pines, in such charming contrast with the rich green of the foliage, by which it is shown off rather than hidden; and, with the green spires of the Firs, they keep the woods warm in winter.

DO NOT OVERLOOK THE SMALLER TREES.

The Yew with its thick green foliage; the wild Guelder rose, which lights up the woods in autumn with translucent glossy berries and many-tinted leaves; or the Bryonies, the Briar, the Traveler's Joy, and many another plant, even humbler perhaps, and yet each with some exquisite beauty and grace of its own, so that we must all have sometimes felt our hearts overflowing with gladness and gratitude, as if the woods were full of music—as if

> **The woods were filled so full with song**
> **There seemed no room for**
> **sense of wrong.**
> **— Alfred Lord Tennyson**

Woodlands are, for some, less beautiful in the winter: yet the delicate tracery of the branches, which cannot be so well seen when they are clothed with leaves, has a special beauty of its own; while every now and then frost or snow settles like silver on every branch and twig, lighting up the forest as if by enchantment in preparation for some fairy festival.

> **By day or by night, summer or winter, beneath trees the heart feels nearer to that depth of life which the far sky means. The rest of spirit found only in beauty, ideal and pure, comes there because the distance seems within touch of thought.**
> **— Jefferies**

IF LAKES ARE LESS GRAND THAN THE SEA, THEY ARE EVEN MORE LOVELY.

The seashore is comparatively bare. The banks of Lakes are often richly clothed with vegetation which comes close down to the water's edge, sometimes hanging even into the water itself. They are often studded with well-wooded islands. They are sometimes fringed with green meadows, sometimes bounded by rocky promontories rising directly from comparatively deep water, while the calm bright surface is often fretted by a delicate pattern of interlacing ripples, or reflects a second, softened, and inverted landscape.

TO WATER WE OWE THE MARVELLOUS SPECTACLE OF THE RAINBOW.

"God's bow in the clouds." It is indeed truly a heavenly messenger, and so unlike anything else that it scarcely seems to belong to this world.

How wonderful is the blessing of color!

When speaking of beauty, birds and butterflies, flowers and shells, precious stones, skies, and rainbows come to mind.

> **Mountains, again, seem to have been built for the human race, as at once their schools and cathedrals; full of treasures of illuminated manuscript for the scholar, kindly in simple lessons for the worker, quiet in pale cloisters for the thinker, glorious in holiness for the worshipper. And of these great cathedrals of the earth, with their gates of rock, pavements of cloud, choirs of stream and stone, altars of snow, and vaults of purple traversed by the continual stars.**
>
> **— John Ruskin**

Who has not sometimes felt "the witchery of the soft blue sky;" who has not watched a cloud floating upward as if on its way to heaven

Sunbeam proof, I hang like a roof
The mountain its columns be.
— Shelley

But exquisitely lovely as is the blue arch of the midday sky, with its inexhaustible variety of clouds.

There is yet a light which the eye invariably seeks with a deeper feeling of the beautiful, the light of the declining or breaking day, and the flakes of scarlet cloud burning like watch-fires in the green sky of the horizon.
— John Ruskin

HOW GRAND ARE
THE WILD WAYS OF NATURE.

How magnificent when the lightning flashes "between gloom and glory."

Ghosts ride in the tempest to-night;
Sweet is their voice between the gusts of wind,
Their songs are of other worlds.
— Ossian

The wonders and beauties of the heavens are not limited by the clouds and the blue sky, lovely as they are.

**The perpetual presence of the sublime."
They are so immense and so far away,
and yet on soft summer nights "they
seem leaning down to whisper in the ear
of our souls.**

— Symonds

As we watch the stars at night they
seem so still and motionless.

Nor is it only the number of the heavenly
bodies that is so overwhelming; their mag-
nitude and distances are almost more im-
pressive. The ocean is so deep and broad as
to be almost infinite, and indeed in so far as
our imagination is the limit, so it may be.
Yet what is the ocean compared to the sky?

These infinities are not only a never-failing
source of pleasure and interest, but seem to
lift us out of the petty troubles and sorrows
of life.

Chapter 17

The Delights of Travel

The fool wanders, the wise man travels

— Old Proverb

It is astonishing how little we see of the beautiful world in which we live.

You can learn about other places from books but that is second rate. When traveling you get to see things with your own eyes.

Adventure is a path. Real adventure – self-determined, self-motivated, often risky – forces you to have firsthand encounters with the world. The world the way it is, not the way you imagine it. Your body will collide with the earth and you will bear witness. In this way you will be compelled to grapple with the limitless kindness and bottomless cruelty of humankind – and perhaps realize that you yourself are capable of both. This will change you. Nothing will ever again be black-and-white.

– Mark Jenkins

The use of traveling is to regulate imagination by reality, and instead of thinking how things may be, to see them as they are.
– Samuel Johnson

Traveling is a great source of knowledge with educational value. You meet different people and visit different places. Get acquainted with new customs and traditions and experience new foods.

People travel to faraway places to watch, in fascination, the kind of people they ignore at home.
– Dagobert D. Runes

Travel is more than the seeing of sights; it is a change that goes on, deep and permanent, in the ideas of living.
– Miriam Beard

To my mind, the greatest reward and luxury of travel is to be able to experience everyday things as if for the first time, to be in a position in which almost nothing is so familiar it is taken for granted.
– Bill Bryson

Traveling is a respite from daily routine and worries.

A good traveler has no fixed plans, and is not intent on arriving.

— Lao Tzu

To get away from one's working environment is, in a sense, to get away from one's self; and this is often the chief advantage of travel and change.
— Charles Horton Cooley

Travel promotes a spirit of brotherhood as it removes many prejudices.

To travel is to discover that everyone is wrong about other countries.

— Aldous Huxley

Perhaps travel cannot prevent bigotry, but by demonstrating that all peoples cry, laugh, eat, worry, and die, it can introduce the idea that if we try and understand each other, we may even become friends.

— Maya Angelou

Travel is fatal to prejudice, bigotry, and narrow-mindedness, and many of our people need it sorely on these accounts. Broad, wholesome, charitable views of men and things cannot be acquired by vegetating in one little corner of the earth all one's lifetime.

— Mark Twain

I have found out that there ain't no surer
way to find out whether you like people
or hate them than to travel with them.
— Mark Twain

Travel encourages us to wonder at our
amazing world.

Wandering re-establishes the original
harmony which once existed between
man and the universe.
— Anatole France

Traveling helps to put things into perspective.

Travel and change of place impart new
vigor to the mind.
— Seneca

One's destination is never a place, but a
new way of seeing things.
— Henry Miller

Traveling engenders feelings of freedom and
newness.

Two roads diverged in a wood and I – I
took the one less traveled by.
— Robert Frost

The advantages of travel last through life;
and often, as we sit at home,

> Some bright and perfect view of Venice, of Genoa, or of Monte Rosa comes back on you, as full of repose as a day wisely spent in travel.
>
> — Helps

So far is a thorough love and enjoyment of travel from interfering with the love of home, that perhaps no one can thoroughly enjoy his home who does not sometimes wander away. They are like exertion and rest, each the complement of the other; so that, though it may seem paradoxical, one of the greatest pleasures of travel is the return; and no one who has not roamed abroad, can realize the devotion which the wanderer feels for Domiduca—the sweet and gentle goddess who watches over our coming home.

> No one realizes how beautiful it is to travel until he comes home and rests his head on his old, familiar pillow.
>
> — Lin Yutang

Chapter 18

The Wisdom of Aging

For I reckon that the sufferings of this present time are not worthy to be compared with the glory which shall be revealed in us.

— Romans viii. 18.

Life is surrounded with mystery. Our world is a speck in boundless space. Our individual livesas wellas that of the whole human race is but a moment in the eternity of time. We cannot imagine any origin, nor foresee the conclusion.

With age you may care less and less, for many things that gave you the greatest pleasure in youth. If your time has been well used, if you have warmed both hands wisely "before the fire of life," you gain even more than you lose. Hope is gradually replaced by memory: and whether this adds to our happiness or not depends on what your life has been.

There are some lives that diminish in value as old age advances, in which one pleasure fades after another, and even those which remain gradually lose their zest; but there are others which gain in richness and peace all, and more, than that of which time robs them.

The pleasures of youth may excel in keenness and in zest, but they have at the best a tinge of anxiety and unrest; they cannot have the fulness and depth that may accompany the consolations of age, and are amongst the richest rewards of an unselfish life.

As with the close of the day, so with that of life; there may be clouds, and yet if the horizon is clear, the evening may be beautiful.

Old age has a rich store of memories.

> **Joys too exquisite to last,**
> **And yet more exquisite when past.**
> **— Montgomery**

Swedenborg imagines that in heaven the angels are advancing continually to the spring-time of their youth, so that those who have lived longest are really the youngest; and have we not all had friends who seem to fulfil this idea? who are in reality— that is in mind—as fresh as a child.

Age cannot wither nor custom stale
Their infinite variety.
— Shakespeare

When I consider old age I find four causes
why it is thought miserable: one, that it
calls us away from the transaction of affairs; the second, that it renders the body
more feeble; the third, that it deprives us
of almost all pleasures; the fourth, that
it is not very far from death. Of these
causes let us see, if you please, how great
and how reasonable each of them is.
— Marcus Tullius Cicero

To be released from the absorbing affairs of
life, to feel you have earned a claim to leisure and repose, is the pleasure of aging.

The higher feelings of our nature are not
weakened with age; or rather, they may
become all the brighter, being purified from
the grosser elements of our lower nature.

Single is each man born into the world;
single he dies; single he receives the
rewards of his good deeds; and single
the punishment of his sins. When he dies
his body lies like a fallen tree upon the
earth, but his virtue accompanies his soul.
Wherefore let Man harvest and garner
virtue, that so he may have an insepa-

rable companion in that gloom which all
must pass through, and which it is

so hard to traverse.

— Manu

The approach of death is a drawback of old
age. To many minds the shadow of the end
is ever present, like the coffin in the Egyptian feast, and overclouds all the sunshine
of life. But ought we so to regard death?

Life, like a Dome of many-colored glass,
Stains the white radiance of Eternity,
Until death tramples it to fragments,
— Shelly

Life need not stain the white radiance of
eternity; nor does death necessarily trample
it to fragments. Man has:

Three treasures,—love and light
And calm thoughts, regular as infants' breath;
And three firm friends, more sure than day and night,
Himself, his Maker, and the Angel Death.
— Coleridge

Death is "the end of all, the remedy of
many, the wish of divers men, deserving
better of no men than of those to whom
she came before she was called.
— Seneca

It is often assumed that the journey to "The undiscovered country from whose bourne. No traveler returns" must be one of pain and suffering. But this is not so.

DEATH IS OFTEN PEACEFUL AND ALMOST PAINLESS.

Bede, the historian, was translating St. John's Gospel into Anglo-Saxon, and his secretary, observing his weakness, said,

There remains now only one chapter, and it seems difficult to you to speak." "It is easy," said Bede; "take your pen and write as fast as you can," At the close of the chapter the scribe said, "It is finished", to which he replied, "Thou hast said the truth, *consummatum est.*"

Bede then divided his little property among the brethren, having done which he asked to be placed opposite to the place where he usually prayed, said "Glory be to the Father, and to the Son, and to the Holy Ghost," and as he pronounced the last words he expired.

Goethe died without any apparent suffering, having just prepared himself to write, and expressed his delight at the return of spring.

We are told of Mozart's death that

**the unfinished requiem lay upon the
bed, and his last efforts were to imitate
some peculiar instrumental effects, as he
breathed out his life in the arms of his
wife and their friend Süssmaier.**

Plato died in the act of writing; Lucan while
reciting part of his book on the war of Phar-
salus; Blake died singing; Wagner in sleep
with his head on his wife's shoulder. Many
have passed away in their sleep. Various
high medical authorities have expressed
their surprise that the dying seldom feel
either dismay or regret. And even those who
perish by violence, as for instance in battle,
feel, it is probable, but little suffering.

Some believe in the immortality of the soul,
but not of the individual soul: that life is
continued in that of our children would
seem indeed to be the natural deduction
from the simile of St. Paul, as that of the
grain of wheat is carried on in the plant of
the following year.

**Millions of spiritual creatures walk the Earth,
Unseen, both when we wake,
and when we sleep,**
— John Milton

The dead exist somewhere else in space, and we are indeed looking at them when we gaze at the stars, though to our eyes they are as yet invisible.

Death cannot be regarded as an evil. To wish that youth and strength were unaffected by time might be a different matter.

> But if we are not destined to be immortal, yet it is a desirable thing for a man to expire at his fit time. For, as nature prescribes a boundary to all other things, so does she also to life.
> — Marcus Tullius Cicero

Weep not for death.

> Weep not for death,
> Tis but a fever stilled,
> A pain suppressed,—a fear at rest,
> A solemn hope fulfilled.
> The moonshine on the slumbering deep
> Is scarcely calmer. Wherefore weep?
>
> Weep not for death!
> The fount of tears is sealed,
> Who knows how bright the inward light
> To those closed eyes revealed?
> Who knows what holy love may fill
> The heart that seems so cold and still.

Many a weary soul will find comfort in the thought that

> A few more years shall roll,
> A few more seasons come.

And we shall be with those that rest asleep within the tomb.

> A few more struggles here,
> A few more partings o'er,
> A few more toils, a few more tears,
> And we shall weep no more.

> Peace, peace! he is not dead, he doth not sleep!
> He hath awakened from the dream of life.
> 'Tis we who, lost in stormy visions, keep
> With phantoms an unprofitable strife,
> He has outsoared the shadows of our night.
> Envy and calumny, and hate and pain,
> And that unrest which men miscall delight,
> Can touch him not and torture not again.
> From the contagion of the world's slow stain
> He is secure, and now can never mourn
> A heart grown cold, a head grown gray, in vain.
> — Shelley.

Most men decline to believe that

> We are such stuff
> As dreams are made of, and our little life
> Is rounded with a sleep.
> — Shakespeare

DEATH FREES THE SOUL FROM THE ENCUMBRANCE OF THE SPIRIT.

There is no Death! What seems so is transition;
This life of mortal breath
Is but a suburb of the life elysian,
Whose portal we call Death.
— Longfellow

We have bodies, we are spirits.
I am a soul dragging about a corpse.
— Epictetus

TO THE AGED DEATH IS A RELEASE.

What might the treasures of Heaven be?

For all we know
Of what the blessed do above
Is that they sing, and that they love.
— Waller

Anxiety of change seems inconsistent with perfect happiness; and yet a wearisome, interminable monotony, the same thing over and over again forever and ever without relief or variety, suggests dullness rather than bliss.

For still the doubt came back—Can God provide
For the large heart of man what shall not pall,
Nor through eternal ages' endless tide
On tired spirits fall?

These make him say,
If God has so arrayed
A fading world that quickly passes by,
Such rich provision of delight has made
For every human eye,

What shall the eyes that wait for him survey
When his own presence gloriously appears
In worlds that were not founded for a day,
But for eternal years?"
— Richard Chenevix Trench

Here there is an infinity of interest without
anxiety. So that at last the only doubt may be

Lest an eternity should not suffice
To take the measure and the breadth andheight
Of what there is reserved in Paradise
Its ever-new delight.
— Richard Chenevix Trench

Let us reflect in another way, and we shall see that there is great reason to hope that death is a good; for one of two things—either death is a state of nothingness and utter unconsciousness, or, as men say, there is a change and migration of the soul from this world to another. Now if you suppose that there is no consciousness, but a sleep like the sleep of him who is undisturbed even by the sight of dreams, death will be an unspeakable gain.

— Socrates

If we are entering on a new a sphere of existence, where we may look forward to meet not only those of whom we have heard so often, those whose works we have read and admired, and to whom we owe so much, but those also whom we have loved and lost; when we shall leave behind us the bonds of the flesh and the limitations of our earthly existence; when we shall join the Angels, and Archangels, and all the company of Heaven,—then, indeed, we may cherish a sure and certain hope that the interests and pleasures of this world are as nothing compared to those of the life that awaits us in our Eternal Home.

Sir John Lubbock

(1834-1913) was distinguished as a banker and man of business, as a zoologist, ethnologist, archaeologist, and as an author and a parliamentarian. He was the eldest son of a baronet, Sir John William Lubbock and a member of parliament from 1870, where he introduced many reform bill. Sir John Lubbock made significant original scientific contributions to entomology and anthropology and published over a hundred scientific papers and twenty-five books. He was considered to have been the greatest educator of his time. The *Pleasures of Life*, from which *Simple Pleasures* was derivied, is among his most popular works.

Dr. Beverly Potter, PhD, earned her Masters of Science in vocational rehabilitation counseling from San Francisco State and her Doctorate in counseling psychology from Stanford University. Docpotter has authored several books about workplace issues that blend the philosophies of humanistic psychology and Eastern mysticism with principles of behavior psychology.

Docpotter has created numerous derivative works from old classics, including *Spiritual Secrets for Playing the Game of Life* derived from Florence Sovel Shinn's *The Game of Life and How to Play it.*

A scene from *Gone With the Wind* is Docpotter's metaphor for her derivitative works. Scarlet wanted to get Rhet back, but didn't want him to know she was poor and desperate. Looking around Tara she found beautiful red velvet drapes, which she cut up to create a stunning red velvet gown, fit for a queen. Docpotter takes the velvet of old classics to create new Works.

Her website is *docpotter.com*. You can also find Docpotter on Twitter, Facebook and elsewhere in cyberspace and the cloud. Please visit.

Timeless Wisdom Series

Derived from Timeless Classics
by Beverly A. Potter

Spiritual Secrets
for Playing the Game of Life
from Florence Sovel Shinn

Simple Pleasures
Tune into NOW!
from Sir John Lubbock

Power of Will
Harnessing the Soul's Capacity
for Self-Direction
from Frank C. Haddock

Tune into
NOW!